The Edge
of the Divine

Other Books by Sandi Patty

Merry Christmas with Love
Sam's Rainbow
Broken on the Back Row
Life in the Blender
Falling Forward
Layers

The Edge
of the Divine

WHERE POSSIBILITY MEETS
God's Faithfulness

SANDI PATTY

THOMAS NELSON
Since 1798

NASHVILLE   DALLAS   MEXICO CITY   RIO DE JANEIRO

Published in Nashville, Tennessee, by Thomas Nelson. Thomas Nelson is a registered trademark of Thomas Nelson, Inc.

Thomas Nelson, Inc., titles may be purchased in bulk for educational, business, fund-raising, or sales promotional use. For information, please e-mail SpecialMarkets@ ThomasNelson.com.

Unless otherwise noted, Scripture references are taken from *The Message* by Eugene H. Peterson. © 1993, 1994, 1995, 1996, 2000. Used by permission of NavPress Publishing Group. All rights reserved.

Scripture references marked NIV are taken from the HOLY BIBLE: NEW INTERNATIONAL VERSION® © 1973, 1978, 1984 by International Bible Society. Used by permission of Zondervan Publishing House. All rights reserved.

Scripture references marked KJV are taken from THE KING JAMES VERSION of the Bible.

Scripture references marked NKJV are taken from THE NEW KING JAMES VERSION. © 1982 by Thomas Nelson, Inc. Used by permission. All rights reserved.

Scripture references marked NLT are taken from the *Holy Bible*, New Living Translation, © 1996, 2004. Used by permission of Tyndale House Publishers, Inc., Wheaton, Illinois 60189. All rights reserved.

Edited by Sue Ann Jones.

Some incidents first mentioned in *Broken in the Back Row* by Sandi Patty. Copyright © 2005 Sandi Patty. Used by permission.

Library of Congress Cataloging-in-Publication Data

Patty, Sandi, 1956–
  The edge of the divine : where possibility meets God's faithfulness /
Sandi Patty.
     p. cm.
  ISBN 978-1-4002-0280-5
  1. Patty, Sandi, 1956– 2. Christian women–Religious life. 3.
Overweight women–Religious life. 4.
Obesity–Surgery–Patients–Religious life. 5. Weight loss–Religious
aspects–Christianity. I. Title.
  BV4527.P3863 2010
  248.8'6196398–dc22

2010009248

Printed in the United States of America

10 11 12 13 14 QG 6 5 4 3

Contents

Indeed these are the mere edges of His ways,
And how small a whisper we hear of Him!

–Job 26:14 NKJV

ONE

The Edge Between Despair and the Divine

I'm on the edge of losing it—the pain in my gut keeps burning. I'm ready to tell my story of failure.

—Psalm 38:19

The doctor's waiting room was nearly full, but painfully quiet. No one spoke. No one made eye contact. We pretended to be engrossed in outdated magazines or busily clicked our smart-phones to check e-mail and text messages. Anything but acknowledge where we were and why.

The door opened, and another woman entered and checked in at the desk, turning in the same sheaf of forms and papers that had taken me nearly an hour to complete. As I had done, she glanced around the room with a tight, self-conscious smile. Perhaps, as I had done, she quickly realized that all the chairs in the waiting room were oversized.

Eventually there were ten of us, as I recall—seven women, three men—and I suspect that the others were feeling the same painful emotions I was. We were embarrassed and ashamed, tormented by the unspoken question: *How could I have let this happen?*

The silence continued, broken only by our phone clicking or page turning. Maybe, as I did, the others stole quick looks around the room, comparing sizes. *Well, at least I'm not as big as* he *is.* About half of them were around my size, I guessed. The rest were larger.

I was relieved to see I wasn't the biggest person there. But it didn't matter, really. We'd all met one terrible requirement that qualified us to sit in that waiting room: we were all at least a hundred pounds overweight.

Later I would laugh, thinking that our size was the painfully obvious elephant in the room. But at that moment there was no laughter. In fact, if someone had asked me so much as, "How are you today?" I probably would have burst out sobbing.

We'd been encouraged to bring along a friend or loved one, but no one did. If the others felt like I did, they couldn't bear the thought of it. We were ashamed to be there, and although the room was full, we felt totally, agonizingly alone. We didn't want our loved ones to share our humiliation as we were forced to acknowledge, in public, how bad the situation really was.

Finally, mercifully, a woman wearing hospital scrubs stepped through an office door. She flashed a warm smile; she'd seen hundreds of us guilty, shame-soaked people sitting silently in those oversized chairs, and she knew what was coming next. She invited us to follow her down the hallway.

After a few steps, we turned into a door leading to the conference room. At the time, I saw no symbolism in that simple movement, passing through a doorway. Now I realize I was crossing an important threshold, stepping over an edge into the unknown.

EDGES EVERYWHERE

The journey I've been on since that spring day in 2008 in the bariatric surgeon's office has been life changing, not only because of the physical changes that have occurred in my body but also because of the enhanced spiritual awareness that journey has given me. A dictionary defines the word *edge* in several ways, but my favorite is "the point at which something is likely to begin." Now when I think about the door of that conference room, that's what I see: an edge where something remarkable began.

Although the doorway seems now, in my memory, like the edge of a cliff, I didn't *fall* over it accidentally. I deliberately chose to step off, not knowing what would happen but trusting God to work it all out for my good, just like Romans 8:28 promises.

I hope you won't think I'm trivializing my relationship with the Savior by telling you in this book how, during the last two years, I lost a lot of weight and gained a lot of spiritual insight. That's truly what happened, and it's simply too amazing not to want to share the story.

I'm encouraged by what Oswald Chambers called "the unexpected sacredness of circumstances." The November 7 essay in his classic devotional, *My Utmost for His Highest*, says, "God by His providence brings you into circumstances that you can't understand at all, but the Spirit of God understands. God brings you to places, among people, and into certain conditions to accomplish a definite purpose through the intercession of the Spirit in you."

Chambers said that God, through the Holy Spirit interceding within us, uses everyday circumstances "to touch the whole world with His saints."

My hope in sharing the story of my weight loss is that you'll be inspired to look for the unexpected sacredness of your everyday circumstances, too, and that you'll find in that sacredness the same closer relationship to the Creator that I've found.

During this weight-loss journey, I've learned that, throughout each day, we encounter points at which something is likely to begin. Edges. My experience, which has included prayer, spiritual meditation, and psychological counseling, has helped me recognize those edges and make better choices—choices that reflect my priorities not only in what I eat but also in so many other things I do.

Sometimes those edges seem insignificant, presenting simple choices: *Should I eat the chocolate cake?* But sometimes even the simplest choices have disastrous consequences or powerful potential. Alcoholics know they're always one little drink away from disaster. Conversely, many of us have seen how a simple word of kindness or the smallest gesture of friendship has had a big impact on someone's troubled heart.

Sometimes big decisions start with small choices: during the invitation hymn at the end of a church service, we may choose to cross a divine edge as we step out from the pew into the aisle. Then, having crossed that edge, we take one step forward, then another, and the next thing we know, we're standing beside the pastor, committing our lives to Christ.

But here's the thing: an edge is the point at which something is *likely* to begin. It may not happen automatically. The edge may be a choice. In this book I want to show you how I've learned to recognize more vividly the edges in my life—the choices that confront me. I invite you to come along on the journey that's teaching me to choose to *act* in ways that confirm what I *say* my priorities are.

My top priority is to love and serve God. To act on that priority, I need to choose actions that honor and care for the body he has given me so I'm able to use it in his service and also use it to cherish and support the wonderful husband, family, and friends he has given me.

It's not always easy to make those choices consistently. Surely we all fail at it. We start a new diet or some other new, healthy habit with great enthusiasm but lose steam as the days roll by. When I was looking at ways the word *edge* was used in Scripture, I found great encouragement in Jesus' words to his disciples in Luke 21:34. He was urging them to keep their enthusiasm for the coming return of God's kingdom, but those same words could apply to so many things in our lives today. He said, "Be on your guard. Don't let the sharp edge of your expectation get dulled by parties and drinking and shopping. . . . Pray constantly that you will have the strength and will to make it through everything that's coming and end up on your feet before the Son of Man." (Don't you just love *The Message* paraphrase of the Bible? "Parties and drinking and s*hopping*"? You'd think those words were directed at women as well as men. Oh! I guess they were.)

When making the right choices feels like stepping over the edge of a cliff into the unknown, it's a scary situation. With experience we learn to take that scary step, make that right choice. We can't know exactly how things will turn out, but we know God is right there with us, and he'll make even the worst things work for our good. When we believe that, we can "stand fearless at the cliff-edge of doom, courageous in seastorm and earthquake, before the rush and roar of oceans, the tremors that shift mountains. . . . God-of-Angel-Armies protects us" (Psalm 46:2–3).

The next time you're confronted with a hard choice, picture yourself standing courageously on that windy, shaky cliff-edge with the psalmist. Or stand beside Moses on the edge of the Red Sea, with thousands of terrified Israelites huddling around you and Pharaoh's furious army thundering down. Or imagine yourself with Gideon and his small three-hundred-man army waiting nervously around the edge of the mighty Midianites' camp, watching for God's signal to attack.

Or . . . come along with me as I step over the edge into that doctor's conference room. At that point in my journey, I wasn't anywhere near the point of standing fearlessly on a windy, shaky cliff. But I *was* about to step over an edge.

Saying Good-bye to Plus-size Barbie

Like many people, I've struggled with my weight forever. Other members of my family have some weight problems, too, although not as serious as mine, so maybe I might have some kind of genetic disposition to heaviness. But after years of therapy, I also know that part of my struggle is connected to something that happened when I was six. I'll tell you about that later. The incident didn't seem to affect my outward appearance immediately. Throughout my teenage and college years, I managed to keep my weight under control. I was never what you'd call skinny, but I wasn't fat either. I was athletic, muscular, thick. I was excited that I was selected as a high school cheerleader . . . until the day I overheard someone say, "You know who Sandi is. She's the heavy cheerleader."

I married young and quickly had four children—two beautiful daughters and a pair of delightful twins, a boy and a girl, in between. While learning how to be a wife and mother, I was also pursuing a very active career in music and was blessed with unimaginable success.

As all those blessings were added to my life, lots of extra pounds were added too. Like many women, I gained too much weight during my pregnancies and then failed to take it off. I went through some serious emotional upheavals—a contentious divorce and a self-inflicted scandal that threatened to end my music career—and through it all, food was my best friend.

Oh sure, I've said that God has always come first in my life, but the choices I was making during those years didn't reflect my priorities. I might have *said* that God was number one, but my choices showed that *food* was my comforter-in-chief.

My weight climbed, and oh, how I fought it. Name a diet, and I've tried it. Name a fitness program, and I've failed at it. The terms *yo-yo* and *roller coaster* don't begin to describe the ups and downs I've put my body through. It's hard enough to go through such successes and failures in private. But as someone who makes a living as a musical performer, mine were right out there for the whole world to see.

I knew that a lot of folks subconsciously think of overweight people as just plain dumb. *Can't you see yourself? Do you know what you look like? Can't you control yourself enough to eat less and get in shape?*

For me, the most common subconscious thoughts about overweight people revolved around personal hygiene. As an overweight person myself, I developed the misguided opinion that *other* fat people seemed to have stopped caring about their appearance. If you had asked me to describe an overweight person, I might have generalized that too many of them seem to stop styling their hair, trimming their nails, and pressing the wrinkles out of their unattractive clothes.

To combat that faulty mental image, and because I am a professional performer, I worked hard to make sure those characteristics *never* applied to me. I knew that in the music industry, an attractive appearance is crucial. Just look at the successful contestants who progress through the levels of *American Idol*. They may start out looking like everyday folks, but by the time they're in the final rounds, the professional stylists have gotten hold of them, and they look spectacular, no matter what size they are.

Through the years I've been blessed to work with professional stylists too. One of them is Ellen Kingston, who is a talented vocalist as well as a stylist. Ellen has worked wonders to make me feel beautiful onstage, especially during the Yuletide series of Christmas concerts I've hosted several times with the Indianapolis Symphony. She found the most gorgeous dresses and costumes for me . . . even in size 26. Without knowing it, she was following the advice of comedienne Anita Renfroe, who advises, "If you can't lose it, decorate it!"

Ellen told me recently that she'd thought of me back then as a plus-size Barbie. With Ellen's help, I felt beautiful when I stepped onstage, even though I knew the audience's first impression of me might not be that I was beautiful but that I was *big*. I believed I needed to work extra hard to win them over, to show them I *wasn't* that dumb, unkempt fat person they might subconsciously categorize me as. I was trying to say to them, *There's so much more to me than what you can see. Just close your eyes and listen to me. I can sing!*

My life as the plus-size Barbie rolled along. I stayed busy as a performer and as wife of my wonderful Don and mother to our blended family of nine extraordinary children (including one amazing son-in-law). I continued to try various diets and programs, hoping to lose weight, but none of them lasted long.

For years I'd heard about surgical weight-loss procedures. During our kids' high school show-choir days, I'd met two other parents, a husband and wife, who'd had gastric bypass surgery. As I recall, they'd each lost something like 180 pounds. They looked fabulous, and I remember thinking, *Wow, that would be so awesome.* I asked them all kinds of questions, and they told me they'd done it because they knew they just weren't healthy. In their huge bodies they really couldn't move around easily and never could have done all the traveling necessary to keep up with their child's many show-choir appearances, they said.

I researched the procedure and even asked my doctor about it. She told me that it's a very invasive surgery. "It's been successful for a lot of people," she continued, "but until you're really ready to make serious lifestyle changes, it's not going to work for you. It's not a quick fix."

Well, I guess what I was hoping for *was* a quick fix. Besides, doctors only wanted to do gastric bypass surgery on patients who were at least a hundred pounds over-weight, and I wasn't there . . . yet.

But I was certainly heading that way.

The years rolled by, and despite all the diets and exercise regimens, my weight continued to climb. I started to hear about a new, less invasive procedure called gastric banding—in particular, the Lap-Band procedure. Curious, I made an appointment with the bariatric surgeon in Indianapolis.

But then I called and canceled it. I just wasn't ready.

Another year or two passed, and during that time, I made other appointments with the surgeon—and canceled them all.

Then I found myself back at my doctor's office for my annual physical. This woman is not only my physician, she's also my close friend. I didn't like the look she gave me as she entered the exam room and looked up from my chart with concern on her face.

"Your weight is up again, Sandi, and your blood pressure too. And your cholesterol isn't good. What's going on?"

I made the usual excuses—a busy work schedule, the demands of being a wife and mother, plus the relatively new stress of worrying how we would put all our kids through college, especially since *five* of them were now enrolled simultaneously.

I mentioned to her that I'd been reading about the Lap-Band procedure. "What do you think?" I asked.

"I have a lot of patients who've been very successful with it," she said. "But, Sandi, it's still not a quick fix. *You* still have to do the work of losing weight. Until you're ready to do that work, it's just going to be another failed attempt for you."

I remember thinking as I heard her words, *It sounds like this weight-loss thing is an inside job, like it has more to do with what's going on inside my head than with what's going into my mouth.*

"I'm seriously considering it," I told her. "But I can't help wondering if . . . well, it almost feels like I'd be cheating God if I do this. He's given me all the gifts I need to accomplish this on my own, but I'm just not using them."

She shook her head as if she were thinking, *Sandi, you just don't get it!* Instead she said, "Sandi, you're still going to need all those gifts. Lap-Band surgery isn't magic. The hunger and all those other feelings that made you eat in the past are still going to be there. That's why I'm saying you have to be ready to make some big lifestyle changes in order for this to work."

Then she said something I'll never forget: "You're not cheating God if you do this. But you *are* cheating your family if you die too soon—and trust me, Sandi, if you don't do *something*, you're going to."

The burning look she gave me underscored the impact of her words.

"Okay," I said, unable to do anything but nod my head and let the tears fall.

She offered to look up the phone number of the bariatric surgeon in Indianapolis for me. I laughed and said no thanks. By then I nearly knew it by heart.

A Glimpse of the "After" Life

The ten of us sat in big swivel chairs around three sides of a large, square conference table, our eyes glued intently on the nurse as she welcomed us to the doctor's office. She talked briefly about height, weight, and body mass index and how, in order to "qualify" for this procedure, we had to be in the medical category defined as "severely morbidly obese."

And that was all of us sitting around the conference table.

That was me.

The awful words seemed to hang there for a moment over my head, and more tears welled up in my eyes. Sure, I'd heard the term before, but never applied to *me*. I thought someone who was severely morbidly obese weighed, you know, six hundred pounds or so. But *me*? Why, I wasn't even half that size. Not quite.

Shocked and ashamed, I fumbled in my purse, looking for a tissue. A box of tissues came gently sliding toward me. Apparently others who'd sat at this table before me had felt the same humiliation and despair after hearing those words. Tissues were a fixture in the conference room.

Mercifully, the nurse quickly introduced a video presentation and turned out the lights. I, for one, was thankful we were no longer on display to each other.

In the video, the bariatric doctor shared another ominous fact: obesity has become America's top medical problem, the cause of more deaths than any other medical condition. Heart disease used to be number one, he said, but medical science has developed medications, treatments, surgeries, and procedures that have reduced that status. Then he asked rhetorically: if you had a heart condition, wouldn't you opt for one of these modern, proven medical options?

Similarly, he continued, medical science has developed the Lap-Band as a proven, minimally invasive procedure to help treat obesity. During the laparoscopic procedure, the surgeon places a band around the stomach that, in effect, makes the stomach smaller. You can still get the nutrition you need through the food you eat, assuming you eat nutritious food, but you can't eat large quantities. Well, you *can* eat large quantities, but you'll pay a hard price for it, usually painful vomiting.

The doctor said it was wonderful how medicine works

hand-in-hand with the body to achieve weight loss. (*And*, I thought, *it's even more wonderful to think medicine can work hand-in-hand with God*.)

Frankly, at that point in the video, the mood in the room hadn't changed. We were grimly watching a report about the statistics that described our terrible medical condition and hearing cut-and-dried facts about the procedure we were about to endure. Then the video's focus switched from the doctor to people like us, everyday folks who expressed the same emotions we were feeling. With the same sad look in their eyes, one after another said things like, "I've tried everything. I've lost and gained and lost again—and then gained it all back plus more." "I know I'm on a path to premature death if I don't do something, but I've failed at everything I've tried." "I'm at the end of my rope. I can't go on like this, but nothing seems to work for me."

Then the video showed us the same people six months later, and there was something different about them. Most of them seemed to have lost some weight, but what I noticed most were their eyes and their demeanor. Somehow they seemed different as they explained that they had had the procedure and had set out on a new lifestyle of healthy eating and exercise.

Then, in the video, we saw the same people a year after their first appointment—a year after they'd sat at the table where we were sitting now. Then they appeared eighteen months later.

The change in them was astonishing. They had lost

impressive amounts of weight, and they were able to do things they'd never been able to do before–or hadn't done for decades. Now they fit comfortably in airplane seats. Now they can climb a flight of stairs, walk a mountain trail, or ride a bicycle.

Amazing.

None of them spoke about their faith, so I couldn't know if they shared my Christian beliefs. But when I heard them describe the change they had been through, Jesus' words in John 10:10 came to mind. These people were now living life "more abundantly" (KJV) than they had before.

With Jesus' help and some assistance from modern medicine, I wanted to live more abundantly too.

The video ended, and the nurse turned the lights on. Everybody sort of peeked around at the others in the room. The most thrilling change had occurred. We made eye contact. We smiled. It was as though we were all thinking, *We can do this!*

As we left the room, some of us actually spoke to each other: "Good luck!" "I hope this works out for you." "See ya later."

There was something different about us now.

Now we had hope.

TWO

Living on the Edge

Now God has us where he wants us, with all the time in this world and the next to shower grace and kindness upon us in Christ Jesus.

—Ephesians 2:7

I sat in my car a moment before turning the key, eyes closed, mind reeling with all I had experienced in the last few days. When I'd gotten out of the car a couple of hours earlier, I'd thought of myself simply as "heavy," or "overweight." Now I knew I was severely morbidly obese. *It just doesn't get much worse*, I decided.

I thought about the changes I'd seen in the Lap-Band people on the video. Then, just as the mood around the conference table had brightened, so did the mood in the car as I pondered, *Could this really be true? Could I really be getting a second chance–okay, a fiftieth chance, given all my previous failures–to start over, lose the weight, and finally become healthy?*

An unexpected image popped into my head of a woman I'd never met but had first connected with many years ago. She had made a mistake so terrible the elders of her village decreed that she was too loathsome to live; they sentenced her to be stoned to death. They brought her before Jesus, named her sin, and reminded him of Moses' law. Then they asked him to confirm her death sentence.

Jesus took his time answering them, but eventually he

must have nodded. "Go ahead," he told them. "The sinless one among you, you go first; you throw the first stone."

You know the story. One by one, the scholars and Pharisees turned and walked away. Apparently they had made mistakes too.

Then it was just Jesus and the sin-scarred woman. She must have trembled as she waited for him to speak again. When he did, he asked her where her accusers were.

In my mind, I see her shrug, maybe wondering fearfully if this was a trick question. "Th-th-they're gone, Lord," I hear her answer.

"You go too," he told her. "Go and sin no more."

This story is my paraphrase of John 8:4–8, and those of you who know *my* story know that several years ago I had good reason to identify with this woman. I *was* that woman! And now I was reconnecting with her in an entirely different way. I was standing there with her, looking up at Jesus in total amazement, whispering, "You mean I get a second chance?"

Looking for a Fleece

That night I talked with my family about the edge I'd crossed, sharing with them the hard, shocking words I'd heard from the two doctors. My husband, Don, and my children all said the same thing: "You don't have to do this if it's just about your appearance. We love you, and we think you're beautiful. But if it makes you healthier and gives you a better chance at living a long, active, and productive life, then go for it. Absolutely. We want to keep you around for a long, long time."

As the days rolled by, I was 99 percent sure I would do it. But there was still one issue to be resolved: the cost. With five kids in private college and another two headed for college soon, Don and I were watching every penny. The doctor's office staff had filed the pre-authorization papers with my insurance company, and now I'd have to wait to see what its response was. If the insurers deemed the procedure medically necessary, I expected they would agree to pay for at least half the cost of the surgery and its related treatments.

In our family we've always tried to stay closely in tune with God, and we watch for signals that he's confirming our path or steering us another way. Our children grew up hearing the story in Judges 6 about Gideon, who was called by God to attack the enemy Midianites—at least he *thought* that's what God was telling him. To make sure he was getting the right message, he asked God for confirmation. He told God he was leaving a wool fleece on the threshing floor overnight. In the morning, if the fleece was wet with dew but the floor around it was dry, then he would know he'd understood God correctly.

Sure enough, the next morning, "he wrung out the fleece—enough dew to fill a bowl with water!" (v. 38).

But what God was asking Gideon to do—attack a much larger army—was a pretty drastic action. Gideon wanted to make sure. So he put out the fleece the next night too.

"Don't be impatient with me," he said to God. "But this time let the fleece stay dry, while the dew drenches the ground" (v. 39).

The next morning, "only the fleece was dry while the ground was wet with dew" (v. 40).

Gideon had his marching orders.

Now, we can't manipulate God or tell him what to do. We may ask him for some signal communicating a message to us, but that doesn't mean he's going to play the game. Still, we can be watchful and prayerful, hoping he will guide our steps in quiet or dramatic ways so that we constantly walk in his will.

The expression "Maybe that's our fleece" is common in our family discussions when we are looking for indications that God's telling us we're heading in the right direction. We still laugh, retelling the story of our family meeting twelve years ago when we were considering adopting a baby. My twins, Jonathan and Jennifer, were eight at the time, and little Jonathan piped up, "Mom, we just need one of those blankets." He was trying to remember the word for *fleece*.

So now I was back in Gideon-mode, watching for a fleece that would confirm that Lap-Band surgery was the right thing to do. I already had pretty strong evidence: being told by doctors that I was severely morbidly obese and headed toward an early death. Still, I was there with Gideon, saying, "Don't be impatient with me, Lord, but I just want to be *sure*." I thought that the insurance company's decision about payment would be that final fleece.

MAINTAINING AN EDGY PERCEPTION

Do you see what was happening to me during this time of decision making? I had just *crossed* an edge, but I was still hovering in its vicinity, still in that free-fall state where I was wondering what was ahead, where I would land. And in the midst of all that wondering, I was staying close to God, watching for his guidance, hoping he would catch me. I was calling out to him more than ever.

Living on the edge isn't always the most comfortable existence, but it's a place where we tend to do more looking around for help—which, for Christians, means looking for God. When we're teetering over a precipice or plummeting into the unknown, we want to know he's right there with us. That's why the edge can be a *good* place to be.

My friend Gene Anderson likes to say, "If you're not living life on the edge, you're taking up too much space!" I think he means you're complacent, set in your ways, maybe a little, well, boring! Instead we need to live life with keen awareness of the opportunities around us, the other edges that might appear that have the potential to bring us closer to the divine. Watching with a mind-set that expects wonderful possibilities to appear in our lives at any moment gives us a whole new perspective on life.

In Andy Andrews's fabulous book *The Noticer*, the character Jones explains this concept to a young man whose circumstances drive him to homelessness. (The scene reminds me again of Oswald Chambers's term the "*sacredness*" of circumstances.") The two men meet under a pier on the beach, where the young man has taken up residency and spends most of his time feeling sorry for himself. Jones–you can't help but think of him as a grizzled old angel–patiently teaches the man to notice things, to see everything around him in a new way: "'So, my contention is that you are right where you are supposed to be.' The old man [Jones] scooped up a double handful of the white sand and let it pour from his fingers. 'It may look like barren sand to you, son, but nothing could be further from the truth. I say to you that, as you lay your head down tonight, you are sleeping on fertile ground. Think. Learn. Pray. Plan. Dream. For soon . . . you will *become*.'"

Living life on the edge means we're constantly at the point where something may begin, or not begin, depending on our *choices*. We're looking around for cliff edges that hover over good futures, praying that God will guide us in choosing the right edges to step off of. But sometimes we misunderstand, or we go charging ahead without seeking God's guidance.

The awful truth is, we make mistakes. Sometimes terrible mistakes.

After we've endured the consequences of poor choices and hard falls, we might be tempted to move back from that cliff edge, huddle in the darkness under the pier, and resume the pity party. But I don't think that's where God wants us. I think he wants us out there on the edge, constantly watching for new opportunities to connect with him more intimately, trust him more completely.

Sure, we make mistakes. That's okay. We're out there with a God who allows do-overs. My friend Max Lucado calls God's grace the "supreme force in salvation." It's what allows us to live life on the edge. Even if we make a mistake and step off the wrong cliff-edge, God's everlasting arms are out there. If we call out to him, believing what he has told us and trusting what he has promised us, he'll pick us up from the rugged rocks below and set us back on the cliff-edge again. It might not be the most pleasant experience we've ever had (and trust me, I've got the "frequent faller" points to prove that I know what I'm talking about here), but God has promised to be with us no matter what and to forgive us when we earnestly ask him to, no matter what.

And he will.

THE FORGIVENESS FACTOR

My friend Max is right. It's God's grace, his promise to forgive us when we ask, that lets us live life on the edge. And it's crucial that we *do* ask. It's equally crucial that, after we receive forgiveness, we then *change*. When we get a second chance, we have to commit to do better next time and not repeat our past mistakes. That was certainly going to be important if I went ahead with the Lap-Band surgery, but it's the same deal anytime we get a second chance.

Choosing to accept forgiveness and take advantage of a do-over means we *have to change*. My friend Dr. Robert Gorrell says that's why "forgiveness truly incorporated into life is all transforming." And that's also why some of us don't accept forgiveness. We say we want a second chance, but if we're honest, we admit that we don't really *want* to change.

Robert tells a powerful story about his own experience with being forgiven. As a young man he attended a Christian college, even though he wasn't a Christian. He found lots of ways to get into trouble, he said. "Probably deep down I *wanted* to fail. I didn't want the responsibility of success."

One night he threw a huge party in the dorm, complete with everything you weren't supposed to have at a Christian college, including liquor and dancing girls.

"Of course, I got caught," he said. The next day he found himself standing before the dean of the school and the dean of students, expecting to be kicked out.

"Instead, they started asking me about my spiritual life," he said. "I didn't have one."

The two faculty members responded by outlining a very strict process by which Robert could remain a student at the college.

Amazed that they would give him a second chance, he said to them, "I don't get it."

"No," one of the men answered him. "You don't. But you need to know you are being forgiven."

With their help, Robert began to absorb the fact that he was *forgiven* but also that he had to *change*. He began a process that would eventually lead to a changed life and a close personal relationship with Jesus Christ.

Did I mention that now Robert is a pastor? He laughs

at the way his second chance turned out. "God has such a sense of humor," he said.

Eventually he served both of those faculty members as *their* pastor, supporting them during critical times in their lives. "You see," Robert says today, "God has this incredible plan of reconciliation for our lives. But it begins with forgiveness."

For those of us living on the edge of the divine, the forgiveness factor operates beneficially on both sides of the equation. When we're the ones being forgiven, we accept that forgiveness, promising to change. When we're the ones forgiving others, we're "trusting that God will work out the justice and healing issues," Robert said. On either side of the process, we learn that we cannot make everything right ourselves; only God can.

Robert points out that God's forgiveness is based on his unconditional love for us and that, when it comes into play out there on the edge of the cliff, it's "demonstrating to the world that there is still hope."

Amen and amen!

SHARING THE GOOD NEWS

We're never alone out there on the cliff-edge, and it's not "just" God that I'm talking about. Look around and you'll probably recognize a lot of other frequent fallers too. (We seem to hang out on the same edges.) We're faced with hard choices, and we're teetering out there on the brink, trying to decide what to do. That's when God might jostle someone like me through the crowd to extend a word of encouragement.

I was given that wonderful opportunity recently when a desperate message appeared on my Web site. I'm editing and paraphrasing here as well as disguising identities, but the basic facts of the story are true.

The message came from a woman I'll call Jane. She wrote, "Sandi, my sister really wants to know if the words of that song you sing, 'I've Just Seen Jesus,' can possibly be true. She says to tell you she has lived a life of sex and drugs, and now she's dying of AIDS and wants to know if God really loves her and cares about her. Her time on earth is almost over; she's slipping in and out of consciousness. I'm playing the song for her now. She says she wants to go to heaven!"

The day Jane's message appeared, I was in Dallas shooting a video for this year's Women of Faith conferences. The schedule was so hectic, I couldn't do anything but take quick glances at the messages being relayed to my cell phone from the Web site and then make hurried, short replies.

Jane's next message told me her sister had spoken with the hospital chaplain, asked forgiveness for her sins, and accepted Jesus into her heart. Hallelujah! She was saved.

But later, when I managed to talk with Jane on the phone, she told me that Kathy was in tremendous pain, and although she was inching ever so close to heaven, she didn't seem able to let go. Jane told me again that the words to the song "I've Just Seen Jesus" were so special to Kathy, but she just didn't seem to be able to accept that they were true. Could God *really* forgive a woman like her?

I asked Jane to hold the phone to Kathy's ear. "Honey, Jesus loves you so much!" I told her. "In fact, you and I are the very kind of women that Jesus loves to love on. There is nothing you could *ever* do to make him not love you."

Kathy's voice was so weak I could barely make out her words. "Home? Jesus?" I thought I heard her say.

"Yes, honey. You can go on home with Jesus," I said. "Right now his arms are outstretched, open wide, waiting for you. He can't wait to tell you how much he has loved you all your life and how special you are to him."

She was quiet for a few moments, and then she whispered, "Jesus!" But this time the word wasn't a question but an exclamation.

"Oh, sweet baby," I said, sounding just like my Women of Faith pal Marilyn Meberg. "He's waiting for you. When you're ready, you just close your eyes and let go. It's okay, Kathy. You can go home now."

Silence filled the miles between us. Then I asked her, "Kathy, when you see Jesus, will you tell him hi for me? Tell him I love him so much!"

"Jesus," she answered so sweetly.

A few hours later, Jane let me know that her sister had stepped over the edge of the divine, into heaven.

What a privilege it was for me to be there on that cliff-edge with Kathy—and not just with Kathy but with Jane too. A few days later, as I was still marveling at the experience we'd shared, Jane wrote again, sharing her own need for forgiveness and her own cliff-edge between choices. I was stunned to learn that Jane was pregnant with a married man's child and felt she had no alternative but to have an abortion. Still, she'd just witnessed the forgiveness and redemption the hospital chaplain and I had assured her sister she had. Was it possible that God might forgive her too? Was it possible that he could forgive her for having an affair with a married man?

About as possible as God being out there on that cliff-edge with her. About as possible as God connecting her to another fallen woman who just happens to be the mother of an adopted son and the wife of a husband adopted as an infant. I had to pause just a second to catch my breath before I could go on. Then I told her, "He absolutely does forgive you, Jane. He already has. And now he wants you to live your life for him. You can't change the past, but you *can* change the future!"

Then I told her about my husband, who was adopted, and our adopted son. "Jane," I told her, "there are lots of couples out there who would love to love your baby! In adoption, one mother gives life, and another mother teaches the child how to live it."

It took awhile for her to answer. Then she said, "Isn't it just like God to take one life but give another?" Thinking about it longer, she agreed that she couldn't take the life of her unborn child and promised to seek adoption counseling.

Thank you, Jesus!

Kathy and Jane were huddling on the edge of despair when God showed up and transformed their circumstances into an edge of the divine. He didn't wait for them to get it all together and clean up their act. He met them there, on the stormy cliff-edge, in the midst of their turmoil, and assured them they were loved and forgiven.

That's my God. That's my Jesus. He doesn't mind getting rained on or mud-splattered. He's right there in the storm with us.

People like Jane and Kathy and me are everywhere among you. In fact, we *are* you—at least we're the imperfect ones among you. We're out there on the cliff-edge, us frequent-faller folks. We're like the shunned woman in Nathaniel Hawthorne's classic novel, *The Scarlet Letter.* She was forced by her community to wear a bright red *A* on her clothing to warn others that there was a sinner in their midst.

Picture Jane, Kathy, and me wearing a big red letter *A* on our shirts too. The fact is, we're *all* wearing one of those big red letters, whether or not we recognize it when we look in the mirror. Maybe you see the letter representing *adultery* or *abortion* or *addiction* or *abandonment*, but if you're a believer, you can forget all those words. For Christians, only one scarlet letter is visible: a big red *A* for *atonement*.

God took our old letter and our old life and replaced it with one of his own choosing. Now we know we've been forgiven. Atoned for by Jesus' death on the cross. Admitted into the kingdom of God, where we are promised grace, mercy, adoration, acceptance, and unconditional love. Forever and ever.

I've thought about this exchange with Jane and Kathy often as I've written this chapter. It keeps bringing to mind a verse from Paul's first letter to Timothy, his evangelist-in-training. Paul wrote, "I'm proof–Public Sinner Number One–of someone who could never have made it apart from sheer mercy. And now he shows me off–evidence of his endless patience–to those who are right on the edge of trusting him forever" (1:15).

What an opportunity it is for us when God puts us next to someone else on the cliff who's "on the edge of trusting him forever." We need to be ready. We need to keep the hotline to God open so we know what to say and what to do to help that person take the next step into the divine.

THE FINAL FLEECE

A few more days went by as I waited to learn what the insurance would pay, if anything, on the costs of the Lap-Band surgery. The doctor's office staff had warned me that it usually took between two weeks and a month to hear from the insurance people. Their experts would evaluate my information and decide if the procedure was medically necessary, and then the company would decide what portion of the bill it would pay.

I'd decided if insurance would pay 50 percent of the cost, I would consider that as the final fleece–God's blessing on the plan. If insurance would pay less than that, or nothing at all, well, then I had some more thinking to do.

About a week after I'd sat at the conference table in the doctor's office, the receptionist left a voice-mail message. I knew it was way too soon for her to have heard from the insurance company, so I was a little nervous about calling her back. Her voice in the recorded message sounded a little strange. "Sandi, call me back right away," she had said.

When I did, she told me first that she'd never heard back from an insurance company so quickly. And then she told me what the insurers had said.

"Sandi, they're going to pay 100 percent," she said.

THREE

Edges, Seen and Unseen

It seems it was good for me to go through all those troubles.
Throughout them all you held tight to my lifeline.
You never let me tumble over the edge into nothing.

—Isaiah 38:16

Lap-Band surgery is a relatively quick procedure performed laparoscopically through small incisions. But even though it's quick and simple, you don't just get the go-ahead from your insurance company and have the surgery the next day. First you have to prepare for the new life you're about to begin. And you have to do some work to figure out how you ended up in the old one.

Mental health therapy has been a godsend to me throughout my adult life. Many times, I've sought out talented and experienced Christian therapists to help me sort through issues that have troubled me. So when I found out that counseling and training were required before the surgery, I was delighted. I wanted to do everything I could to make this fresh start successful.

That pause before having the procedure let me gather insights that would help me succeed after the surgery. The work was beneficial not just in helping me learn to eat less and adopt a healthy lifestyle but also in giving me a fresh perspective on the blessings I've received and the challenges I've faced. I gained fresh confidence and enthusiasm that have increased my endurance and lifted my spirits. By sharing a little of my story, I hope you'll be inspired to look at your life, too, and gain insights from recognizing the blessings and challenges you've experienced.

GROWING UP IN MUSIC

I can't remember a time when music wasn't an integral part of my life; I think it somehow was melded into my genes. My mother is a fabulous pianist, and my dad has an amazing voice. They've both spent their adult lives working in music, usually in church ministries but also traveling with musical groups.

As a young man, Dad traveled all over the country singing with the Pennsylvanians, a popular musical group directed by Fred Waring, known as "The Man Who Taught America to Sing." They sang everywhere from state fairs to the White House.

Wherever we lived during my childhood, Mom was usually the church pianist, and during church services, my brothers, Mike and Craig, and I were often parked on one of the pews near the piano so Mom could keep an eye on us while she played. She also taught piano lessons in our home.

My parents tell me that my first public performance occurred when I was two and a half. Dad lifted me up to stand on a table at the church we attended, and I wowed the congregation with a rousing chorus of "Jesus Loves Me" (at least that's what my parents say, but then, they might not have been the most objective people in attendance).

Not too long after that, Mom bought me a little record player that I could play with all by myself. While I don't remember standing on the table and singing "Jesus Loves Me" for our church family, I certainly remember that little record player. I spent many, many happy hours playing musical nursery rhymes, children's Bible-story songs, and all sorts of other music. I sang along, danced, and performed elaborate musical pantomimes for enthusiastic imaginary audiences—or for my parents when they had time to watch.

Now I sometimes think back to all the pleasant hours I spent alone with that little record player, and I can see that I've always loved performing whether or not anyone was watching. In fact, early on as an adult making a career of music, I remember feeling a little amazed that people seemed to like watching me do what I liked doing so much.

Marinated in music and surrounded by love, I was a happy child.

As soon as Mom and Dad decided we were old enough, my brothers and I started performing in churches with our parents as the Ron Patty Family. During the summers our family toured America in a rented RV that pulled a trailer loaded with everything needed for a concert—lights, sound equipment, a piano, an organ, and a drum set, including the big kettle drums my brother Craig played, and even a platform we used as a stage that Mom would trim with a roll of bright fabric. We wore outfits coordinated around our purple theme color, and frankly, we were *awesome*.

Not braggin'. Just sharin' my testimony, as my pal Chonda Pierce would say.

An Unexpected Abuser

By the time my family was traveling the country together on our summer tours, I was a happy, busy teenager who enjoyed school and had lots of friends. On the outside, it looked like I had a perfect life. I certainly had all the components of one: wise and loving parents, rambunctious younger brothers whom I adored, a stable home life, and a solid foundation of faith.

But something terrible had happened to me when I was six: an abusive, secret event that has impacted my life to this day. I wrote about the incident in more detail in my book *Layers*. As many abuse victims do, I kept it secret because I was convinced it had been my own fault and because I was filled with shame; I believed I had caused it to happen.

The incident occurred when my parents were away for several days with a traveling musical group and left me with a trusted church friend and schoolteacher we all knew and respected. She had been warm and friendly toward me throughout our family's previous friendship with her, but that changed as soon as my parents drove away from her house, leaving me behind in her care.

During the nights while I was staying at her house, the woman abused me. She did not hurt me, but she touched me in ways that traumatized me. As a compliant six-year-old, I was confused by what she was doing but was too scared to tell her to stop. I was terrified, but I kept my eyes closed and pretended to be asleep.

The abuse continued nightly. During the day, while I was at her home and whenever I was in her class at the elementary school where she taught, the woman was cold and distant toward me. I was a good kid. I never got in trouble, except in this teacher's class. Sometimes she would come by my little desk and unexpectedly lean down to say harshly, "Sandi, you go stand in the corner."

"Why?" I would ask, completely surprised. "What have I done?"

"*You* know," she would hiss.

Standing there in the corner of my classroom, my face to the wall, humiliation sending hot tears rolling down my cheeks, crazy thoughts swirled in my head: *I didn't do anything wrong! But clearly I did, because she's the teacher and she said I did. Is she talking about those nights at her house? But that was her fault. No, it must have been my fault because she's an adult and I'm just a little kid. She knows way more than I do. If she says I'm a really bad person, then that must be true, but what did I do? Why am I bad?*

I needed someone to talk to, someone who could help me figure out the terrible mystery and identify the abuse for what it was. Someone who could help me set aside the shame that would haunt me for decades. I was too young to see the hard edge I had crossed—no, not crossed. Rather, I'd been pushed over it by someone who had harmed me. On that dark side of the hurtful edge, I would move forward into the years ahead trailing a heavy weight of unjustified but devastating guilt and shame.

The best thing for me at that point would have been to tell someone what had happened. Receiving help, counseling, and reminders of my parents' (and God's) unconditional love for me would have helped me get back to the other side of that edge of evil. It would also have focused blame on the abusive babysitter.

But I was afraid to tell anyone, terrified to let anyone know what a bad person I was. I certainly couldn't tell my parents! They were wise adults, like the babysitter. If they knew what had happened, they would of course side with her, and they might even punish me more.

Such are the thoughts of a child who's been the victim of abuse. They don't make any sense at all—unless you're the child who's been victimized.

The memory makes me think of another event that is totally unrelated but illustrates my thoughts and behaviors as I hovered unknowingly along that childhood edge. In July 1999, before the single-engine airplane John Kennedy Jr. was piloting crashed into the ocean off Martha's Vineyard, it behaved in crazy ways. Radar records show that the plane banked steeply and then dove straight into the sea at great force.

Why would John Kennedy do such a thing? For the same reason a six-year-old abuse victim does the crazy thing she does—thinks the abuse is her fault. From what I've read, Kennedy was an experienced pilot—but not experienced enough. He might be thought of as a "child" pilot.

Experts say that on that hot, hazy July day, he lost the horizon; it simply wasn't visible to him in the thick, fog-like haze. He couldn't see the edge where the sky met the water, and he didn't have enough experience to trust the airplane's instruments, which were telling him he was steering his airplane into the sea, heading toward disaster. Instead, he trusted his *feelings*, which were telling him he was doing the right thing.

Similarly, after the abuse, I trusted my six-year-old feelings rather than the "instruments" my parents had established for me: They had taught me the difference between right and wrong. They had taught me it was wrong for one person to hurt another without justification. They had told me I could always tell them anything and everything.

But I was a little girl lost in a fog of confusion. I couldn't see the edge I had crossed. I "looked" at the instruments my parents had given me, just like we assume John Kennedy looked at the instruments in his cockpit. But I didn't believe them. I believed what I was *feeling*, and my feelings told me I was dirty, shameful, and bad. I kept the abuse secret for nearly forty years.

A Terrible Secret's Terrible Impact

As an adult, I finally recognized the truth that I'd been an innocent little girl who'd had an awful thing done to me. But there just didn't seem to be a reason to bring the horrible history out into the open. Now I know, thanks to all the counseling I've received, how that terrible secret impacted my thoughts and behaviors as it smoldered within me all those years.

For one thing, I see now that over the years I turned to food as a source of comfort whenever tension arose or troubling thoughts and behaviors occurred. Counseling has helped me understand how that has happened.

Like many abuse victims, I've struggled with an illogical, subconscious attitude about my appearance. The fact is, while many of us are using food for self-comfort, we're also subconsciously saying such things to ourselves as, *I can't let myself look good. After all, I was really cute and little when I was six, and look what happened to me. If I'm not cute, if I'm heavy and cumbersome, maybe bad things won't happen to me again.*

Sure, this all sounds crazy to you if you've never been through an abusive situation. But let me tell you, those vows are powerful. When you vow, completely subconsciously, never to be pretty again, you set yourself up for a lifetime of destructive habits, including overeating.

It's common for abuse victims to seek out people who help us accomplish our subconscious goal, either through judgmental criticism or by joining us in our destructive behavior–which just shows how blessed I've been to have Don in my life. From the beginning of our relationship and no matter what my weight has been, he's told me in a whole host of ways that I am beautiful. It took me a long time to believe him; I simply thought that God had given him special eyes. I didn't quite know how that had happened, but boy, was I thankful for such a miracle.

Before Don entered my life, however, my journey took a lot of crazy twists and turns. There's a country song, "Bless the Broken Road," that describes how God blessed a crooked, unlikely life path that led one person straight to another. Looking back, I'm thankful for the convoluted journey that brought me to my life today. I'm *not* thankful for the abuse and still don't understand why it happened. But I can see that God has worked everything that's happened to me for good, just as he promised to do.

One of the things he worked for good was a defining edge in my life that seemed like a weight-related disaster at the time but turned out to be a divine appointment for the future.

A Disney Dream Dashed

I was born in Oklahoma but also lived with my family in Arizona and California; I attended junior high and high school in San Diego. During those teenage years, I went to Disneyland in nearby Anaheim so many times I actually got bored with it.

Back then you could buy a one-day ticket that didn't include riding the rides but allowed you to walk around, shop, eat, and take in all the different shows. That was perfect for me; I spent many happy days going from one musical show to another. I knew all the words to all the songs and had a special fondness for the group called the Kids of the Kingdom.

When I graduated from high school, my one and only dream was to work at Disney and be part of that group. I couldn't wait until I was eighteen, the minimum age to audition. When that day finally came, I hurried to Anaheim and quickly learned the little dance the show's staff taught the auditioners. I wasn't the best dancer, I have to say, but I had grown up singing. I knew I could do *that*!

Each of us did the little dance and sang for the "judges" while all the fifty to seventy-five others in the audition group sat around us along the four walls of the room. When my turn came, I watched the judges' faces while I sang and felt a surge of confidence when I saw them begin to smile. One judge turned down the corner of my application paper, which I took to mean he wanted to remember me. When I finished enthusiastically singing "Don't Rain on My Parade," the room erupted in applause. I left the audition feeling sure I was a shoo-in for the group.

The staff had told us we would be receiving something in the mail in a few weeks, and I rushed to the mailbox every day, looking for my acceptance letter. Nothing came from Disney. Three weeks, four weeks went by. Still nothing.

Finally I called the information number and asked if perhaps my letter had gotten lost in the mail. The woman who answered the phone asked me to hang on for a minute while she checked. My heart pounded, and I nervously chewed a fingernail as I waited for her to check the records. Then my face broke into a smile when she came back to the phone and said, "Oh yes, Sandi Patty. I remember you. What a voice!"

Whew! I thought. *My acceptance letter just got lost.*

But then the woman continued. "However, your dancing was a little weak, and we felt like you were carrying a little too much weight," she said. "I'm sorry, Sandi; we just can't use you."

I was stunned. I was crying before I even hung up the phone, and then I cried all day. And the next day and the next. My parents watched me mourn the death of my dream and tried everything they could think of to encourage and comfort me. But I wouldn't even come out of my room.

Finally Dad slipped a little note under my door. I still have it today. It said, "Today, I watched my little girl transform from a caterpillar into a butterfly." He went on to say other loving things, including how proud he was to see me handling a great disappointment with such maturity.

Was he kidding? Crying hysterically and locking myself in my bedroom didn't seem very mature to me! But now that I have children of my own, I remember that event through a parent's eyes, and I see that Dad was offering me a little lifeline of encouragement to help me get back on my feet and get on with my life.

LIFE IN THE BRIAR PATCH

Not getting accepted into the Kids of the Kingdom felt like a big, loud *NO!* from Disney. It was as though I'd been pushed backward over a devastating edge that separated me from my dream and sent me into no-man's-land.

But that no-man's-land turned out to be my briar

patch. Remember how, in Joel Chandler Harris's classic Uncle Remus tales and recreated in Disney's *Song of the South*, Brer Fox is considering how he will kill Brer Rabbit? Brer Rabbit begs him not to throw him in the briar patch: No, no, no! Anything but that. Oh-please-oh-please-oh-please, don't throw me in the briar patch!

The way Uncle Remus told the tale, Brer Rabbit was the smart one, and Brer Fox was the one who got duped. The fox threw the rabbit into the briar patch, thinking he was killing him in the most horrid way imaginable when, in fact, he was sending Brer Rabbit home. He *lived* in the briar patch!

How many times do we beseech God for something, sure that we know what's best for us? *Oh-please-oh-please-oh-please, God!* But in our story, the roles are reversed from Uncle Remus's version: God is our all-knowing Creator, and we're the ones being duped by our own self-centered and narrow-focused pleas. We think we know what's best for ourselves, and we beg God to give it to us. But sometimes God does what *he* knows is best for us, even while we're begging him to do something different. Even when the divine thing he's doing looks like devastation through our limited earthly eyes.

Heartbroken and hopeless after Disney's rejection, I decided to leave California and attend one of our church denomination's colleges, Anderson University in Indiana. I thought I would become a music teacher. Pretty boring, compared with a career performing at Disney. But that seemed to be the only option left to me.

So there I was, living in the briar patch of Anderson,

Indiana. It wasn't the Magic Kingdom, but I managed to cope, and I was determined to stay busy. I signed up to sing with campus and church groups and, to earn spending money, I started teaching piano lessons.

One of the rabbit trails there in the briar patch led me to two giants in the world of Christian music, Bill and Gloria Gaither. They lived in Indiana and had strong ties with Anderson University. Gloria called me one day and asked if I could take two of her kids as piano students. "Of course!" I answered.

After we got to know each other, the Gaithers asked if I could do some work for them in their recording studio, singing backup with vocal artists and groups and also singing commercial jingles their studio did under contract.

Although I was working as a singer, I'd learned my lesson about setting my hopes on a musical performing career. For one thing, I knew that performers were constantly facing audition situations, and I'd already seen how much it hurt to be rejected from something you'd set your heart on doing. For another thing, I'd seen how much my dad's secondary career with musical performing groups had taken him away from his family. I'd also lived through the consequences of what could happen when parents' careers took them away from their family. I didn't want that for my future family.

All those reasons confirmed that giving up my dream of being a musical performer was the right choice for me.

Still, whenever opportunities arose, I jumped at them. Now that my brothers were older, my parents were often out on the road again, traveling with other groups, and

whenever they came near Anderson, I joined them to perform a song or two.

Then one day Bill Gaither called and asked me to be
a backup singer on an upcoming tour the Gaithers were
planning.

It took me a second to grasp what he was saying. Bill's
words seemed too good to be true. *Travel with the Gaithers,
one of the best-known groups in the history of Christian music?
Are you kidding?!*

"Bill, let me pray about it. *Yes!*" I shrieked.

I traveled with the Gaithers for several years. Sometimes the Gaithers' concert lineup would include a song or
two I sang by myself. One of them was Dottie Rambo's
masterpiece "We Shall Behold Him," which in 1982 earned
Dottie the Dove Award for Songwriter of the Year.

That same year, the Dove Awards for Female Vocalist of
the Year and Artist of the Year went to an eager young singer
from . . . well, her bio said she lived in Anderson, Indiana,
but you and I know she came from the briar patch, a place
she ended up after begging God to send her somewhere else.

STILL TOO FOND OF FOOD

Except for a short interlude (I temporarily transferred back
home to San Diego State, mostly due to homesickness), I
lived in Anderson thirty-five years. I finished college and got
married there. My children were born there, and my parents
moved there after their retirement. My career soared while

I lived there–so much for deciding I didn't want to make a career out of performing!–and then plummeted when my own poor choices caused churches and Christian radio stations to shun me.

Throughout all these happy times and heartaches, food continued to be my favorite way to celebrate the good times and my preferred source of comfort when things were falling apart. I gained too much weight with every pregnancy and then lost too little after each baby was born. I used food to stuff my feelings when the criticism came.

Yes, I'm a Christian. Yes, I have a personal relationship with Jesus. Yes, I know he's able to share our joy and heal our heartaches. I know, I know, I know. But when tensions rose and my feelings were hurt, my willpower and self-control seemed to falter. Jesus seemed far away, and that candy bar was oh, so handy.

Then there was that other thing, the continuing psychological impact of my childhood abuse.

PEERING OVER THE EDGE OF THE BALCONY

At the height of my career, when I'd won more Grammies and Dove Awards than I'd ever dreamed possible, my marriage ended. While it was in its death throes, but before the court finalized the divorce, I fell in love with Don Peslis, a handsome, talented singer who performed with my backup group during national concert tours.

For a while it felt like I had a multitude of full-time jobs, including being a mom to four adorable live-wire children, maintaining a busy performance schedule so that I could support my family, and doing everything I could to keep the press from finding out what was going on behind the scenes.

When my husband and I separated, I looked for a new church. It just seemed too awkward, too stressful, to keep showing up each week in the same congregation but sitting in different pews and forcing the kids to sit with one or the other parent. So one Sunday I ventured out to a new church. I left the kids in the nursery and slipped up the stairs to the balcony, hoping no one would recognize me. I was exhausted, both physically and emotionally, by everything that was happening in my life, all the pressure and stress, plus the constant fear that my scandalous secret would be exposed and the world as I knew it would come crashing down on me.

I settled into a seat on the back row, thankful for the large crowd around me that helped me feel anonymous. I hoped no one would recognize me or try to talk to me. I felt so alone. So lost. So ashamed of my mistakes.

As the music started, so did my tears. I soaked up as many as I could with the one tissue I found in my purse. After that, I let them fall uninterrupted. Through the hymns, through the offering and communion, through the sermon and into the introduction of the invitation hymn. Then the pastor, Jim Lyon, stepped off the platform and into the aisle. With sunshine streaming through the stained-glass window above me, I had to be backlit. He couldn't have seen my tear-stained face peering back at him over the edge of the balcony. But the words he said seemed to fly like an arrow right to me.

"If you're visiting with us today, we're so happy to have you here," he said. "There are people all around you who would like to know your name, if you would like to tell them. We want you to know that the God we serve lives within these walls—and outside these walls too."

He took a few more steps down the aisle and looked all around the crowded sanctuary. "But maybe you're visiting us here this morning, and you're not ready to tell anyone your name. Maybe all you want to do is sit on the back row of the balcony and cry. That's okay," he said. "We want you to know that the God we serve knows how to find you there. He hasn't forgotten about you. We serve the God of second chances, the God of new beginnings. We serve the God who sets his children free."

For a moment I couldn't catch my breath. *Was he talking to* me? Furtively, I looked around. I certainly didn't see anyone else sitting on the back row of the balcony crying her eyes out. It was a big church, and he was so far away, and I knew the light had to be shining in his eyes. . . . Still, his words echoed in my mind.

When the service ended, I hurriedly gathered the kids out of their classrooms and herded them into my car. As I drove home, their happy chatter buzzed around my head as I tried to process what had happened.

We serve the God of second chances, the God of new beginnings.

I started regularly attending North Anderson Church

of God, and there I learned the truth of the words Jim Lyon spoke that first Sunday I attended. I *did* make a new beginning there, starting with a long, complicated process of reconciliation that included regular meetings with accountability partners and a public acknowledgment of my situation to the Sunday church congregation.

Jim Lyon, who's now my close friend as well as my trusted spiritual adviser, assured me he *hadn't* seen me crying in the balcony that first Sunday. He wasn't speaking directly to me—or at least solely to me. He was simply saying what God put on his heart to share at that moment. And wouldn't you know God would give him exactly the right words to reach the woman he couldn't see but sensed was there. That's my God, all right!

Many months later, having asked forgiveness and completed the long course of reconciliation, I knew my relationship with God was stronger than ever and my relationship to the church had been restored. In August 1995, Don and I were married, and I was happier than I had ever been. The edge of the balcony had been, for me, the edge of the divine. Just like Pastor Lyon had said, God found me there and gave me a second chance. I had started a new life and was determined to keep Christ at the center of it.

Yet, ironically, that was when the whole sordid story of the scandal I had caused finally appeared in the national press.

In response, churches canceled concerts; radio stations stopped playing my music. Recording plans were put on hold. I was criticized, condemned, ostracized.

And once again I found myself crying out to God: *Oh-please-oh-please-oh-please, Lord, make this hard, ugly stuff go away. Calm my critics. Let them see the deliberate and humiliating steps I've taken to be restored to your church. Help them understand that I've repented; remind them that Christians are forgiven people. Make them stop, Lord!*

But once again, God had other plans.

FOUR

Finally Valuing My Value

We find ourselves standing where we always hoped
we might stand—out in the wide open spaces of God's grace
and glory, standing tall and shouting our praise.

−ROMANS 5:1

I've always been intrigued by people who lose weight when they're slammed into some tumultuous or traumatic situation. Apparently there are actually people who lose their appetite in the face of grief, stress, and anxiety. In contrast, trouble usually sends me right to the kitchen in search of my old friend, Food. For me, there's nothing quite as comforting as a plate full of warm chocolate chip cookies.

I spent a lot of time in the kitchen after the Christian music world found out about the improper way my relationship with Don had begun. The phone stopped ringing, bookings were rare, and harsh words were plentiful. The great irony was that by the time the details were made public, I'd gone through the yearlong reconciliation and restoration process with the help of my church. I had asked for and received forgiveness by everyone directly impacted by my poor choices. But it took a long time–years–for those facts to make their way through the more tantalizing tabloid-style criticisms.

Some folks still haven't gotten the good news–or have

chosen not to believe that someone could be forgiven for sins as serious as mine.

Sure, I was hurt by the harsh reaction, and I worried when my career took a nosedive. But there were many good things about that time too. With my career at a standstill, I was able to be at home to enjoy uninterrupted time with my new husband and our blended family of seven wonderful children. Oh, the fun we've had together! Oh, the adventures we've shared!

Being married to Don for nearly fifteen years has been amazing and wonderful. He nourishes me in so many ways: he supports me, entertains me, and loves me no matter what. Every day, with those special eyes God gave him, he has looked at me and told me I was beautiful.

Out in the world, I wore that same old wardrobe of secret shame. But Don made me feel . . . well, there was a part of me that couldn't quite believe what I felt–*Can he really feel this way about me?* The truth was, he made me feel *cherished.*

During my counseling sessions before the Lap-Band surgery, I got a glimpse of the future, when it might be possible for me to finally believe that I'm pretty, even through ordinary eyes. That kind of thinking doesn't happen because you get some kind of "extreme makeover, personal edition." It doesn't happen because you lose weight. Actually, you can adopt that mind-set even if your appearance doesn't change at all. Liking what you see in the mirror comes when you realize that *you have value* as a living, breathing human being.

The weight-loss counseling was secular, but I've had enough Christian-based therapy to understand that Christians have an extraordinarily powerful reason to believe we have value. Our whole faith is grounded in the fact that God himself came to earth and endured unimaginable agony on our behalf. He did it not just on our behalf collectively but on behalf of each of us individually. Even if I'd been the only person on earth, Jesus would still have done it. He would have come to earth and gone through the crucifixion just for *me*. Overweight, emotionally scarred Sandi. And for *you*.

And remember. Jesus didn't go through that ordeal so that we could merely survive. He said he did it so we could "have life, and that [we] might have it more abundantly" (John 10:10 KJV). Or, as the *Message* version puts it, so that we could have "more and better life than [we] ever dreamed of."

If we can just believe that, we can understand that we are *priceless*. And if we have such great value, we're certainly worth the effort to take care of ourselves and to do whatever we can do to have that life that's better than we ever dreamed possible. Eventually, such thinking brings us to believe that we're worth the cost, headaches, and challenges of something like Lap-Band surgery, which helps us take a big step toward that healthy life God wants us to have.

Filtering the secular weight-loss counseling through the framework of my Christian beliefs brought me to the same bottom line that applies to anyone trying to break old habits and develop a new, healthy lifestyle: I would never make a lasting change in my destructive thoughts and behaviors until I believed I was *worth* the change, worth whatever effort it took to *make* the change.

Gradually, I accepted that fact. I began to allow myself to hear that message—not just from Don but also from God.

On the other side of that edge, that new way of thinking, dramatic changes were waiting.

CHANGING MY CHOICES

I kept coming back to that point of realizing weight loss is an inside job. It's ultimately more about *thinking* than *eating*. That's why I'd failed at the dozens of other weight-loss diets and programs I'd tried. I just hadn't been convinced that I was worth the effort to endure whatever it cost me in time, money, or sacrifice. The old shame and the old way of thinking would come sneaking back in, and once again I would fail.

Analyzing it now, I believe I would lose weight pretty steadily until I got to a point where things got scary. Then maybe that old, ridiculous-but-common abuse victims' fear would rear its evil head, and I would subconsciously think again, *Oh, dear. I'm starting to look pretty good. But if I look good, bad things may happen to me again.*

All those old illogical thoughts and feelings were going to be right there waiting for me after the surgery. The same physical hunger, the same dumb tendency to use food to

comfort myself in the face of stress, hurt, worry, embarrassment, whatever–all those feelings would still be there too.
But now I was learning a new way to recognize and respond
to them. I was learning how to feel pretty again, learning to
feel the value God gave me–and you–when he created us.

Today, nearly two years after the whole process began
around the doctor's office conference table, I still fight
those feelings. But the help I've received related to the Lap-
Band surgery has given me a lot of new insight and wisdom
about my relationship with food. It has trained me to pause
before I take that second bite of cake and ask myself, *Do you
really want to do that, Sandi?*

I heard repeatedly during the preparatory sessions that
my stomach would be a fraction of its former size, but I
could still *choose* how much I ate. Having a smaller stomach
(actually my stomach would remain its usual size, but the
Lap-Band would make it act as though it were much smaller)
wouldn't keep me from feeling hungry, either physically or
emotionally. I could still submit to my habit of using food
for self-comfort when I felt tense. And I could still eat a
full-size meal.

But it was drilled into my head that it takes most of
us twenty minutes to feel full. If I ate slowly and reduced
the amount I was eating, that pleasant feeling of fullness
would most likely occur while I still had food on my plate.
The counseling sessions taught me to recognize the feeling
and enjoy it.

If I ate the old way–hurriedly, either at meals or in that
old, familiar reaction to tension, shoveling it in without

really thinking about the food itself–the feeling of fullness would come too late, and it wouldn't be a good feeling at all. More than likely, the too much food I'd gobbled down was going to come back up pretty quickly. *That* certainly wasn't a "pretty" image at all!

My Second Birthday

At a Women of Faith conference last year, I complimented a woman about how good she looked. She said thank you and then leaned in closer and said something like, "You should have seen me a couple of years ago. I've lost nearly two hundred pounds."

"Wow!" I answered. "That's amazing. How did you do it?"

She almost whispered her answer. "Well, I didn't do it on my own. I don't know how you feel about this, Sandi, but I had gastric bypass surgery."

I grabbed her hands. "Yes, you *did* do it on your own. I had Lap-Band, and I know *we* still have to do the hard work. It's still hard, isn't it? We still have to watch what we eat and exercise and stick with all those lifestyle changes, but now . . ." I stopped and hugged her. "Can you believe we've done this?"

She told me she now celebrates two birthdays: the day she was born and the day of her surgery. "Because that's when I got my second chance to live a healthy, productive life."

I so get that!

My own second birthday came on August 26, 2008, nearly five months after I crossed that first edge that set me on this course. I'd had hours and hours of counseling and lifestyle training, and all sorts of physical tests to make sure I would be able to tolerate the anesthesia and the rest of the surgical components. I had been traveling with the Women of Faith tour almost every week of the summer, but the upcoming Labor Day break would give me time to recover from the procedure. So the surgery was scheduled, and this time there was no way I was backing out of that commitment.

Knowing the surgery was coming up on Monday, I spent that last weekend in August performing and speaking at a Women of Faith conference, all the while planning the food orgy I would have on Sunday before beginning my new life on Monday. What I was planning was something like a breakup party with food. I was going to have one last food fling and then behave myself forever after. I flew back to Indianapolis from Women of Faith Saturday night and stopped at the grocery store as I was driving home from the airport. Let's see, tomorrow I would feast on bread and pasta and ice cream and cake and . . . Oh, it was going to be spectacular.

Then, before I went to bed Saturday night, I read the pre-op instructions. Perhaps you thought I would have read them long before that, but that's just not how I operate. My mouth fell open as I read what the paper said: I had to *fast* the day before the surgery. Clear liquids only.

What was I thinking? Of *course* you have to fast before surgery! There would be no breakup party with food. Instead, I wrote food a breakup letter. It went something like this:

Dear Food,

I want to thank you for being my friend all these years. My relationship with you has been the longest, most enduring relationship I've ever had; you've always been there for me, from the very day I was born. I grew up and left home, but you stayed right there with me. Every day and every night, you've been my source of strength and comfort, the thing I turned to in every celebration, every moment of boredom, every painful challenge.

But, Food, I'm breaking up with you. I feel like you've turned on me, and I don't like the way you define our relationship anymore. In a healthy relationship, one doesn't take advantage of the other. Each one benefits in a healthy relationship. There are healthy boundaries and healthy solutions during difficult times. And none of that is happening in our relationship now. Instead, you're constantly whispering to me, "Come here, come here."

You used to be my faithful supporter, Food, and now you're a domineering tyrant. You don't care about me anymore; you don't want what's best for me. So I'm saying good-bye, Food. We'll still be friends, but I'm taking control of the relationship. I'm calling the shots now, setting the boundaries.

There's a new sheriff in town, honey, and it ain't you.

Amazingly, I slept well the night before the surgery. I'd expected to maybe have trouble falling asleep or to toss and turn as I contemplated the next day's agenda. Instead, I snoozed soundly. I wasn't nervous at all. In fact, I was eager to take that next step and cross that next edge. All the counseling and training sessions during the summer had prepared me well, and I was looking forward to beginning the new life awaiting me on the other side of surgery. So I closed my eyes, said my prayers, and slept.

But I didn't sleep long. We were up early so I could be at the hospital on time. Don drove me from our home in Anderson to Indianapolis, about an hour away.

During the pre-op preparations, I asked the anesthesiologist for a special favor. I explained that I made my living with my voice and I'd heard there's a relatively new way of administering anesthesia during surgery that doesn't involve inserting a tube into the patient's throat. I asked him if he could please use that method, and he agreed to do so, as long as there were no complications.

With that settled, Don and I shared a prayer while I waited for the surgical team to come get me. When they did, he sweetly kissed me good-bye and wished me good luck.

As I was wheeled away to the operating room, another thought unexpectedly came to my mind. I remembered sitting with the psychologist back in the surgeon's office during one of the preparatory sessions. She was going through the personality test I'd taken and was sharing some of the findings with me, noting that the test results indicated my strengths as well as my weaknesses.

Throughout my test, she said, she saw one trait appearing repeatedly, and that trait was *resilience*. I'd been through a lot of challenges, she said, and again and again I'd shown great resilience.

Yes, I could see that. I've taken a lot of knock-down punches, but with God's help, I keep getting back up.

The doors to the surgical suite closed behind me. And the next thing I knew, the procedure I'd been preparing for since March had finally been done. This resilient woman had crossed the edge into an amazing new life.

FIVE

Seeking the Lost, Cherishing What's Found, Releasing the Excess

Imagine a woman who has ten coins and loses one. . . .
When she finds it you can be sure she'll call her friends
and neighbors: "Celebrate with me! I found my lost coin!"
Count on it—that's the kind of party God's angels
throw every time one lost soul turns to God.

—LUKE 15:8–10

B ack in 2005, Don planned a special surprise for me as we celebrated our tenth anniversary. As bookings at Christian venues had dried up, I'd looked for other ways to continue my career, and as a result I was doing more work singing with metropolitan symphonies. That, in turn, had led to more work that had a patriotic theme. Gradually, my career started regaining some momentum.

Don was attending graduate school in San Diego that summer while I was back home in Indiana with the kids. I had been invited to do a concert at a military base in Hawaii, and I was flying through San Diego to meet Don. Then he would continue on to Hawaii with me, both to sing with me in the concert and to celebrate our anniversary.

Don is great at many things, but the man *cannot* keep a secret, especially when the secret is something good. When a happy surprise is in the plans, he just can't wait to share it. He had secretly bought me an anniversary gift, planning to give it to me in Hawaii on the day of our anniversary. But like I said, he simply can't keep a secret, and he can't wait to share something good.

Lucky for me!

I arrived in San Diego and had an overnight stay before we flew on to Hawaii. That night Don took me out to dinner. We had agreed that we would celebrate our important days by exchanging meaningful greeting cards. With the number of kids in our blended family, there wasn't a lot of room in the budget for Mom and Dad expenditures, and both of us were fine with that.

Besides, Don has always *loved* good greeting cards. You know that guy standing in the card aisle of the drugstore who's reading all the cards and crying? Yeah, Don's that guy. He loves to pick out just the right card for someone, and he likes receiving special cards as well.

So I had carefully chosen a special card for him, and he'd picked out one for me. I'd stuck mine in my purse that evening, knowing Don's inability to wait. I'd thought, *Sure, our plan is to celebrate our anniversary in Hawaii, but I won't be surprised if he gives me my card tonight.* So I was prepared.

We enjoyed dinner at a nice restaurant, and sure enough, as we were lingering over coffee and dessert, out came Don's card. I can't remember, all these years later, what the card said, but I'm sure it was absolutely perfect for the occasion. Then I handed him my card, and he read it carefully, absorbing every heartfelt word.

The waiter came, and Don asked for the check. Just as I was thinking the evening was coming to a comfortable conclusion, Don reached in his pocket and said, "Oh, yeah. One more thing."

Then he pulled out a little box and handed it to me.

Inside was the most beautiful diamond ring I'd ever seen. (Some things *are* better big!) Instantly I thought, *Can we afford this?* But I didn't say it. I just trusted that Don knew what he was doing. I ecstatically slipped the ring on my finger and leaned across the table to give him a huge kiss. It was *gorgeous!*

I wore the ring for five or six months, and each time I looked at it I realized again how lucky I was to have Don in my life. I loved it when people noticed the ring, because I could tell them what a sweet and thoughtful husband I had. "It was a surprise," I would say giddily.

One day I took the ring off to take a shower as I was hurrying to pack and get ready for a weekend trip. I put it somewhere in the bathroom–somewhere I would be sure to remember it and where it also would be safe from falling down the drain.

And then, can you believe, when I looked for it again a few minutes later, it was gone! It had vanished. Disappeared. Simply evaporated into thin air.

Well, okay, the truth is, I'd forgotten exactly *where* I'd put it in the bathroom so it would be safe and I would remember where I'd put it. I frantically tore the bathroom apart, looking everywhere I could think to look–and folks, it's not that big a bathroom! But I could not, for the life of me, remember where I'd put it, and despite my best efforts, I could not find that ring. I had a plane to catch, so I couldn't spend much time looking for it, but believe me, the time I did spend was intense.

I couldn't bring myself to tell Don what had happened.

I kept hoping, throughout the weekend away, that when I got home I could take my time, go through the bathroom, drawer by drawer, shelf by shelf, and find the missing ring. That's exactly what I did but without success. I finally came to the grim conclusion that somehow the ring had been thrown away—either by me as I hurriedly packed for the trip or by Don, unknowingly, during the time I was away. It was a crushing thought. *How could I have been so careless with something so valuable?*

Weeks passed, and occasionally Don would ask me, "Hey, where's your ring?"

I would look down as if taken completely by surprise. "Oh!" I would exclaim. "I forgot to wear it. Sorry, honey. You know how I love that ring."

Finally, months later, I confessed what had happened, and I apologized for being careless with such an expensive gift.

Don gulped, his eyes widened, and all the color disappeared from his face. But that's all that happened. That's just how he is. Like me—and *with* me—he's made mistakes. He understands that accidents happen. Yelling at me and blaming me for being careless weren't going to help matters. He probably wouldn't have done either, even if it *had* helped. We regretted the loss but moved on. I bought discount store jewelry. Really, Target has some nice stuff, and I've decided the cheaper it is, the brighter the bling.

Several months went by, maybe a year and a half. Then one day I walked into our bathroom, and the ring was lying on the counter by the sink. I screamed. And shrieked. And cried. And then screamed some more. I ran out of the bathroom, out of the bedroom, up and down the hall, down the stairs, in and out of the kitchen, screaming and crying, so happy I simply couldn't contain myself.

For a moment, my family probably thought maybe I'd somehow had my own personal Rapture experience and was in some kind of pre-departure happy-hysteria mode. Either that, or Publisher's Clearinghouse had miraculously shown up in our bathroom to announce that I'd won a million dollars a day for life.

To lose something I valued so much had been crushing. Embarrassing. Frustrating. I had spent hours looking for it, shed tears regretting its disappearance. And then, to find it again . . . the joy was simply indescribable.

What happened was, we'd hired a company to come in and give our house a thorough deep cleaning. The crew came in and cleaned out the dirt that hid under and behind furniture and in the corners and crevices that didn't get cleaned during regular weekly cleanings. God bless that honest but unknown crew member who cleaned my bathroom, found the ring–I don't know where–and left it there, waiting for me, on the counter.

I vowed to take better care of the ring and be more mindful of where I put it.

And I did. Every time I took the ring off, I mentally told myself, *I'm putting the ring in the blue box, and I keep the blue box in the third drawer of my dresser.* That kind of thing.

Then, about six months later, I was on the road somewhere. I wore the ring during a performance and came back to my hotel room that night and carefully put it in a bag and put that bag in something else and put the something else in some part of my luggage. Apparently I forgot that crucial step of deliberately saying to myself where I was putting it. All I could remember when I got home was that I'd put it somewhere that I wouldn't forget.

I'd lost the ring again.

LESSONS LEARNED, RELEARNED, AND LEARNED AGAIN

Life is a continual learning process, and many of the lessons are downright painful. It doesn't help that we have to repeat some of the hardest ones again and again. I was bereft, realizing I'd lost the beloved ring again. *How could I be so dumb? Where on earth did I put that ring?*

I went through every piece of clothing, every box and bag in every piece of luggage. Turned the suitcases upside down and thumped on the bottoms. Once again, the ring had disappeared.

I wore my Target jewelry. I rarely lose a ring, necklace, bracelet, or earring I've bought at a discount store. Why is that?

The story of my lost ring seems completely trivial in light of losses suffered by so many, especially in these difficult times for our nation. So many people have lost loved ones in war, lost jobs, lost their health, lost their family's stability. As I'm writing this book, the news is full of stories about the thousands of earthquake victims in Haiti who lost *everything* in the blink of an eye.

Such losses line up along hard edges of unimaginable sorrow and grief in our own minds, and many of us think we simply could not survive them. We marvel at those who do.

All these thoughts and images have swirled through my mind recently, and I want to learn the lessons they have to offer. Seeing the televised reports of a fallen soldier's funeral, hearing a worried father describe what's happened to his family since he lost his job, weeping as I watch the news reports from Haiti, I'm reminded of Jesus' lessons to us about what is really important.

One of those lessons appears in Luke 10:38–42, which tells about a visit Jesus and his disciples made to the home of a woman named Martha and her sister Mary. During that visit Mary "sat at the Lord's feet listening to what he said." Martha, in contrast, scurried around the house "distracted by all the preparations that had to be made" (NIV).

We don't really know the details, including how many of Jesus' disciples were with him, but we can make some assumptions. The picture I get from these limited facts is that the guests had dropped in unexpectedly, and Martha was frantically trying to serve the group some quick refreshments while also picking up the clutter, getting the beds ready in case they ended up spending the night, and then assembling enough food to feed what might have been a dozen or more hungry men.

Whew! Just thinking about it wears me out. Apparently Martha was having to do all the work single-handedly because her silly sister wasn't lifting a finger to help. Mary was sitting in there with the company, looking doe-eyed at their friend Jesus and hanging on his every word as if her life depended on it. No wonder Martha was cranky!

She probably gave Mary all sorts of silent signals, maybe gesturing impatiently from a doorway behind Jesus' back. *Would you* puh-lease *come in here and help me?* her look might have said.

But Mary completely ignored her sister's increasing frustration and remained totally focused on Jesus.

Finally Martha couldn't keep quiet any longer. She marched into the living room and snapped at Jesus–whined to the One who had single-handedly created the whole world. "Lord, don't you care that my sister has left me to do the work by myself?" she fumed. "Tell her to help me!"

It's so interesting to me to read the way Jesus responds to her. His words to Martha resonate down the centuries to point out the most essential priority any of us should have, even today: "There is only one thing worth being concerned about. Mary has discovered it, and it will not be taken away from her" (v. 42 NLT).

Jesus' words are profound, yet he shares them so simply, with kindness and gentleness. He doesn't shout with dramatic arrogance. No, we have to look for the crucial lesson in his simple reply; we have to stop and listen carefully, and absorb what he's saying. We can only hope that's what the distracted Martha did too.

In every Bible version I can find, Jesus' answer begins with the patient tone of a wise and loving teacher.

"Martha, Martha," he says to her. We imagine him smiling and shaking his head a little as he looks into her eyes with wisdom and love. Some translations have him saying, "My dear Martha," or "Martha, dear Martha."

In contrast, many of us might have replied, "Duh! Don't you get it, you lame-brained moron?" (Well, I hope none of us would have *really* responded that way, but knowing what we know now, that's what we might have thought!) The Lord's answer to Martha clearly identifies what our number one priority is supposed to be. His words give us the perspective we need in order to understand what's really important: *Jesus is the most valuable "possession" we can ever have–because he gives us the hope we need to survive the loss of everything else.*

Making Jesus our first priority makes it easier to categorize the rest of our lives. When we filter everything through our focus on him, we see our blessings as gifts and our hardships as challenges that draw us closer to his sustaining love and strength.

And the best thing is, once we've found Jesus we can never lose him. We find him by confessing our sins to him, asking him to forgive us, and then believing what he says is true. Doing so sweeps us over the edge of the divine into the Savior's arms, where he promises to hold us for all eternity.

CHERISHING THE GIFTS WE FIND WITHIN US

The last couple of years have been remarkable ones for me as I've made this journey from "morbid obesity" toward good health. The counseling and training I've received, in addition to previous mental health therapy, has been tremendously helpful, not just in losing weight but in maintaining a healthy perspective on my life.

For one thing, it has helped me realize the importance of journaling so that I can look back on the journey I've taken and remember how God has guided me, corrected me, rescued me—how he's always been there for me. Sometimes as I scan back over the words I've written in my journal, I feel like the Israelites must have felt, standing in the promised land and looking back at the altar of stones they'd built on the banks of the Jordan River.

God told them to take stones out of the Jordan and use them to build the altar so that in the future, when their children asked why the stones were there, the Israelites would be reminded to tell them the story of how God had been faithful to bring them to the land he had promised them. God had stopped the waters of the Jordan that day so they could cross, just as he had rolled back the waters of the Red Sea when they were fleeing from Pharaoh.

God directed the Israelites to remember the story and tell it to their children "so that everybody on earth would recognize how strong GOD's rescuing hand is" (Joshua 4:24). That's what journaling does for us. Later, when we review what we wrote, we remember our story—and see God's hand at work in our lives. And we trust him to work in us and help us again.

Another thing therapy has done is give me fresh perspectives on nearly everything. One of those perspectives is what some people describe as a constant "attitude of gratitude," one that makes us constantly aware that every good thing in our lives is a gift from God.

In his book *The Noticer*, Andy Andrews's grizzled old character Jones teaches someone how powerful this attitude can be. "The seeds of depression cannot take root in a grateful heart," he says. I read Andy's book last fall as my band and I toured the country on a Christmas concert tour. I'm blessed to work with talented people whose strong Christian faith shows me they have their priorities in order. As I looked back over my journal and simultaneously mulled over the gifts I'm grateful for, I thanked God yet again for the people he's brought into my life. And I thanked him for the love of music he planted in my heart so long ago.

When I was a tiny girl singing and dancing to the musical Bible stories and nursery rhymes I played on my little record player, music was just a way of entertaining myself. Later, as I faced heartbreaking hurts and overwhelming challenges, music became my therapy. When I couldn't find the words to describe the hurt I was feeling inside, music became the heartfelt expression of my pain. It was my silent plea for help, begging God to surround me with his love and strength.

What an extraordinary gift music has been for me.
Thank you, God!

A Dream Outside the Window

When I think back to that little girl playing music on a record player in her bedroom, I see an edge, a point at which something was likely to begin–and *did* begin. My love of music and the joy I've found in performing it have been a blessing that brings me ever closer to the divine presence of God. What a thrilling and rewarding life journey it's been, and in many ways it began when my mom bought that little record player and set it up for me in my bedroom.

Think about the blessings in your life, large and small, and see if you can pinpoint that edge when each one was "likely to begin." Sometimes it's fun to remember and then to realize how a rewarding career or an enjoyable talent got its start. Can you see yourself teetering on an imaginary edge back there in your memory? Was there a point where something simple happened that set you on your path?

As I started thinking about my own "edgy experiences," I wanted to hear how others discovered or identified their gifts and talents. These thoughts were working in my mind during last year's Christmas tour, when I was spending long hours on the bus with my band members. One by one, they told me about their stories, and each seemed to include a simple moment when they crossed a significant edge and stepped out on a journey that would put their gifts on display for all to see as they freelance all over the continent–and beyond–working with other singers and bands in a wide range of music and performance events.

Maybe, as you read their stories, you'll be inspired to

consider your own talents and gifts and identify that edge where they first became apparent. And then, if you're like me, you'll have a deeper sense of gratitude toward the One who gave you that gift and helped you find it in such a creative way.

My friend and colleague Ellen Kingston, the stylist who thought of me as the "plus-size Barbie," is also a very talented stage performer who graciously steps off the stage occasionally to work with me behind the scenes when I need her.

Although she didn't recognize the edge of her performing career when it happened—few of us do—Ellen "found" her gift as a little girl, lying in her bed at night in her family's Wisconsin home. During the summer, with her bedroom window open, she could hear the sweet, lilting sounds of a little-theater production in the pavilion of the park across the street. She especially remembers being swept up in the sounds of the waltz during the classic musical *Carousel*.

"I remember thinking, *Oh, I so want to do that!*" Ellen told me.

Ellen grew up in what she describes as a *Leave It to Beaver*-style family, except it was nearly triple the size of television's Cleaver clan. Ellen's parents had seven children instead of the Cleavers' two, and money was tight, but Ellen, the fifth of the seven children, didn't know it. Her parents often volunteered for community theater productions (something fun to do that didn't cost any money).

Inspired by her parents' work in the theater, as well as by the beautiful memory of the "Carousel Waltz" that wafted through her bedroom window, Ellen happily staged her own childhood song-and-dance shows. When you have six brothers and sisters, she said, you can always find an audience. In those little "home shows," she found the love of performing that would become her lifeline later, as an adult, when her marriage fell apart and she found herself living in the briar patch, a place that didn't look at all like the happy home she'd hoped God would give her.

Looking around for a way to support herself, Ellen fell back on the talents God *had* given her, the ones that came so naturally to her. She built a successful career around her beautiful voice as well as her other talents in the performing arts. She's performed and starred in many theatrical productions, and it seems apparent now that her career path began in the strains of the beautiful music that wafted in from beyond the edge of her windowsill.

STIX'S STORY

Steve (Stix) Hanna's career as a percussionist may have begun with an edge-of-the-divine moment on the day his parents bought him a little toy drum set when he was barely three years old.

Steve's parents worked in music–his dad was director of the band at Depauw University, and his mother sang in the church choir. Apparently *they* noticed early on that their son had a good sense of rhythm and a feel for music.

But Stix himself grew up wanting to be the next "high-dollar Major League Baseball player," he said.

He *was* good at the sport. He remembers being thrilled that as an eleven-year-old he was invited to play on the twelve-year-olds' team. His parents encouraged him to take percussion lessons then, but he balked. He thought baseball was his gift.

Ah, but God has such interesting ways, doesn't he? Every evening after baseball practice, Stix would come home and head for his bedroom, where by now he had a full-size drum set. "I'd close the door and spend the rest of the night playing my drums to my dad's big-band records," he said. (*Ah, another record-player kid*, I thought, hearing him say that.)

Steve's "point at which something was likely to begin" was actually a gradual progression. Over time, his love for baseball faded, but his love for music never did. It's how he's made his living and supported his family for more than thirty years.

He said something interesting as we were talking about edges and my work on this book. He noted that a life-edge isn't always a sharp, defining line. Sometimes it becomes apparent as your interest in one thing wanes and your passion for something else grows. There's no instruction manual for recognizing each new edge we encounter, Stix said. We simply ask God to be with us on the passage and to guide us in our decision making. Then we step out in faith, believing we'll end up right where God wants us to be.

Obviously, Stix Hanna did exactly that. Just consider

some of the stars he's worked with: Roger Williams, Johnny Mathis, Andy Williams, and the late Henry Mancini, to name a few.

ANOTHER MUSICAL ROOMMATE

My musical director Steve Potts's career-edge moment came the same way Stix's and mine did: when his parents set up something musical in his bedroom. For Steve, it was a Steinway grand piano!

Maybe you think Steve's parents were simply wealthy and indulgent and that buying a Steinway grand was no big deal. Well, you're thinking wrong, sister. Steve's dad was a truck driver who also worked in the truckline offices. His mom stayed at home with Steve and his younger siblings and sometimes worked for Sears. Around 1970, when they bought Steve the piano, probably with borrowed money, it cost seven to eight thousand dollars, about half their total yearly income. (By comparison, Stix remembers that his first car, a brand-new 1973 Dodge station wagon, cost three thousand dollars.)

Steve's parents not only bought him the piano, they also gave him the biggest bedroom in their modest ranch-style home so that he and his new piano could be roommates! I tease him now that they put the piano in his bedroom so they didn't have to listen to him play it. He agrees that was probably a big part of their reasoning, but he also knows that having the Steinway in his room made all the difference. "If it had been out in the living room, I never would have had the chance to get alone with it–shut the door and fall in love with it," he told me.

Steve insists that he didn't have any particular gift (we'll dispute that thought later). He says he was simply a compliant child who went along with what his parents wanted him to do, which was learn to play the piano. They loved music themselves, especially country music. "They thought the Grand Ole Opry was the greatest thing on earth," Steve said.

His extended family gathered regularly at Steve's grandma's house for what they called hootenannies, and Steve played his grandma's old upright piano during the family's country-music jam sessions.

His parents wanted him to enjoy other kinds of music too. He remembers, as a young boy of maybe eight or nine, riding sixty miles through a North Texas ice storm because his parents wanted him to hear renowned classical pianist Van Cliburn in concert in Fort Worth.

Even before Steve recognized it himself, his mom and dad obviously saw the gift God had given him. Then one day, after a couple of years of taking lessons and practicing alone in his bedroom, Steve remembers a truly edge-of-the-divine moment, when he recognized his gift. It came when he was sitting at the piano, thinking about a song he'd heard, and he realized, *I can figure this out. I know how that song goes.*

As if by magic, he knew the notes to play. Now, nearly forty years later, those notes are still there, he says, "under my fingers."

I love imagining that moment when Steve sat at that keyboard as a teenager and realized the song in his head was also there under his fingers, just waiting for him to play it. That moment was a beautiful edge of the divine when his connection to God and his blessings became apparent. That spark ignited a passion that still blazes, decades later, as Steve uses his music to glorify God in his career and in his life.

It makes me wonder now what's there, "under our fingers" or somewhere within us, that's waiting to be revealed to us as a beautiful gift from God. Be alert to those edges! Watch for those extraordinary moments when something divine is "likely to begin" in your life.

By the way, Steve still has that Steinway. And incidentally, one of his daughters went to college on a piano scholarship!

Steve's remarkable career as a pianist has him performing in a variety of musical settings, from his local church to Carnegie Hall. But he hasn't forgotten his country-music roots. During the writing of this book, I was asked to sing two songs at the Grand Ole Opry while the band and I were performing in Nashville.

I had never appeared at the Opry, and I was a little hesitant because I wasn't sure the Opry audience would go for my kind of music. But when Steve heard about it, he quickly said, "Oh, you *have* to do the Grand Ole Opry because *I* have to come and play for you. My family will be so proud."

So we did. And they were.

THE GUN SHOP CONNECTION

There's one more remarkable story about the way a band member recognized the divine edge when a career in music was likely to begin. The rest of us can trace our careers back to our childhood bedrooms. But bass player Randy Melson's edge-of-the-divine moment happened in a gun shop!

When he was about ten, Randy saw the Beatles perform on the old *Ed Sullivan Show*, and he was shocked by what he saw. "It took my breath away," he said. "I was just taking everything in—the music and the way the girls were screaming."

A few days later, in the back of a comic book, Randy found an ad promoting greeting card sales as a way kids could make money. He signed up—and sold enough cards to earn fifty dollars, an enormous sum back then.

He'd seen a guitar in the window of a local gun shop, apparently one the owner had taken in trade. With cash in hand, he asked his dad to go with him to buy it, a beautiful Sears Silvertone that came with its own amplifier, all in one case.

Inside the shop, Randy remembers that he was messing around with the guitar, trying it out (he didn't even know how to play it yet), and "a couple of little girls went walking by and looked in through the door at me."

The gun shop guy nodded toward them and then looked at Randy and raised his eyebrows, as if confirming what the ten-year-old wannabe guitarist was thinking himself: *See? That guitar is a bona fide girl magnet!*

Randy remembers that edgy moment like it happened this morning.

Pretty soon it became apparent that the music was just waiting for him there, under his fingertips too. Randy is completely self-taught, which confirms the gift God gave him long before he even realized he had it. He has been supporting himself and his family for more than forty years with that God-given gift and a deep love for music.

CHERISHED "FINDS"

What a wonderful gift music has been for us throughout our lives. We cherish it and thank God for every note we've been able to sing, hum, play, or hear. We're living proof of Proverbs 16:3: "Put God in charge of your work, then what you've planned will take place."

I've been blessed with so many other gifts to enjoy, appreciate, and use. But I must mention the two most profound "finds" I've experienced during edge-of-the-divine moments. Both of these stories are told in detail in my book *Broken on the Back Row*, so I'll just mention them briefly here. I don't want to repeat things you may have read elsewhere, but when I'm talking about cherished *finds*, these two have to be included.

During the months leading up to our wedding, Don and I kept tossing around the idea of adopting a child after we were married. But whenever we mentioned the idea to anyone, the response was almost always the same: Are you crazy? You already have seven children!

Still, we talked about it from time to time. Don was adopted at birth by a loving and devoted couple; his adoptive dad died when Don was young, and Don had mentioned several times to me that he'd often thought how great it would be if he could someday adopt a child and name him Sam, after his adoptive dad.

To make a long (and wonderful) story short, one day, when we had been married about six months, out of the blue, the phone rang. It was one of my friends, Shari, asking if we knew anyone who knew anyone who might consider adopting a baby that her lawyer husband was involved with as a legal representative. She was *not* asking us if *we* would consider adopting the baby. After all, as she knew perfectly well, *we already had seven children.*

But we *did* consider it. After a day or two went by, we went so far as to ask to see the newborn. My friend and her husband took us to the hospital to make the visit, and as we sat in the car in the parking lot, Shari insisted that we pause and ask God to give us some kind of convincing sign—a burning-bush kind of sign, she called it—that would tell us his will for us.

Then Don and I sat in a waiting room while Shari and her husband went to get the baby from the hospital nursery. Later, when they came pushing the little plastic bassinet, Shari was crying, unable to speak. All she could do was shake her head and wave toward the baby.

I knew the baby had endured some difficulties during

delivery. I feared that Shari's tear-streaked face and fumbling gestures meant some serious problems had developed.

But it turned out she was crying tears of joy, and as the little group came closer, I could see what her awkward gestures were about. It was the little sign taped to the bassinette. It was a name tag. The nurses had given the baby a temporary name when he was born.

They'd named him Sam.

Oh, my! Just remembering the day now, fourteen years later, brings joyful tears to *my* eyes. Sam is now taller than I am and wears a size 11 shoe. He is a smart and delightful boy, just like his two brothers, our sons Jonathan and Donnie. We cherish all of our children, of course. But while the others came naturally, we feel like we "found" Sam when he was on the brink of being lost in the foster-care system.

Thank you, God!

The second "find" occurred as Don was searching for his birth parents. His adoptive parents had both died, and he felt a yearning to know the rest of his own story. Unfortunately, by the time he identified who his birth mother was, she had died. But her relatives carefully, and a bit hesitantly, gave him what clues they had to guide him in his continued search for his father.

Finally, after much seeking and a roller-coaster ride of hopes and disappointments, the day came that the phone rang and Don heard his birth father's voice for the first time. What a moment that was.

Since then Don's dad—we call him Pop—has become a wildly beloved and completely cherished member of our family, even living with us for several months at a time. Don has gotten acquainted with his siblings, and wonderful things have happened. It's been amazing.

Maybe the most poignant moment came when Don went to visit his dad in West Virginia for the first time. That night, after he'd gone to bed, he heard a knock on his bedroom door. It was Pop, carrying a glass of milk and a plate of cookies. He'd come to tuck Don in and tell him a bedtime story. He'd never gotten to do it when Don was a boy growing up, he said, and he wanted to make up for all those boyhood bedtimes he'd missed. Another cherished moment.

RELEASING WHAT WAS NEVER NEEDED

I *cherish* the many gifts God has given me, and I've *found* a lot of blessings throughout my life. But when it comes to "cherishing" the extra pounds I "found" every time I looked in the mirror–forget it!

Now that I'm nearly eighty pounds lighter (maybe more by the time this book is published), I'm careful to say that I haven't *lost* that extra weight. Saying I've lost it implies that I want it back. And believe me, I don't! Instead, I've *released* those extra pounds. I've sent them on their way, and I don't *ever* want to find them in the mirror again!

SIX

Hanging on the Cliff-Edge

You pulled me from the brink of death,
my feet from the cliff-edge of doom.

—PSALM 56:12

O n the evening after my surgery, Don brought me home, and I began my new job: getting healthy. If I hadn't been thoroughly prepared beforehand by all the counseling and training sessions. I might have been tempted to think, *Whew! The hardest part is over.* But now, educated and motivated, I knew that wasn't the truth. The hardest part–but also the best–was just beginning.

That evening was a little strange. I'd just had this life-changing surgical procedure, yet there I was, at home with my family, and everything just sort of unfolded like it did every night. Three kids were living at home then–Mollie, Erin, and Sam–and my dear friend Carolyn Gill had come from Florida to help cook and keep the household running while I recuperated. The other kids called or came by to see how Mom was doing.

I made a brief appearance to assure everyone I was fine, and then I headed upstairs. After scrawling a quick note in my journal, I crawled into bed. I hadn't actually "done" anything myself, but the effects of the anesthesia, plus the fact that we'd gotten up in the middle of the night to get to the hospital on time, meant an early bedtime for me. I remember smiling before I dozed off, thinking I was making a new beginning, a fresh start. *This is what God's grace feels like*, I mused. *Thank you, God!*

I had about ten days off before the next Women of Faith conference, and the first three or four days post-op required a liquid-and-soft-foods diet—broth, pudding, soups—while I recovered from the surgery. I wasn't hungry, but I'd been told that condition would be temporary, a result some people have after anesthesia. The hunger and the impulse to eat when I wasn't hungry, all those overeating issues I'd struggled with before, were still out there, waiting to challenge me again.

Gradually, I began eating "real food." But since the surgery I eat differently than I did in my former life. Before, I would eat until my plate was empty, usually distracted by conversation or something I was reading or watching. Now I eat deliberately, sensing each flavor and texture. I still enjoy dining with friends and family, of course, but I try to focus on one thing at a time, shifting back and forth between what's being said and what I'm eating.

When I'm ready to focus on the food, I pick up my fork and look at what's on my plate to pick the very best bite I can find. I know I won't be taking too many bites, so I want to make each one count! For instance, if I'm eating a cheese-and-vegetable omelet for breakfast, I'm going to look for the bite in that omelet that has as many of the flavors together as I can find: a little cheese, a morsel of broccoli, a chunk of tomato, a tiny piece of bell pepper.

I'm not digging around on my plate like I'm excavating for gold. If I were your breakfast partner, you probably wouldn't even notice. Well, you might *now*, after I've told you how I've learned to eat. I just take an extra moment to *look* at my food, focus on it enough to decide where I'm going to stick my fork, and then select the best possible bite. I *really* enjoy that bite. I put down my fork and take an extra split second to think about the flavors I'm tasting.

In between bites, I *really* concentrate on the people I'm with and the conversation flowing around me. I'm simply more aware of every part of the meal than I was before.

Immediately after the surgery, I was instructed to take a bite, put down my fork, chew *twenty-five times* (try it sometime; it takes awhile!), swallow, and then wait a moment. The pauses were designed to help me recognize the increasing feeling of fullness.

I don't drag out the process so extensively now that I'm several months down the road, but I'm definitely eating more slowly. And that's crucial. I have to keep in mind that essential fact about it taking twenty minutes for the stomach's sensation of fullness to get to the brain. Which is a little strange, when you think about it, because the stomach's chronic cravings for a hot fudge sundae seem to happen almost instantly, don't they? I need to stretch out the time I'm taking for a meal so that I take fewer bites during those first twenty minutes of eating. Otherwise, with my new tiny stomach, I'm in a big mess of trouble!

Every morning during that recovering time, I would get on the scale and, no kidding, I had lost a pound or two or three since the day before. The diet is *so* restricted there at the beginning that the weight just seems to vanish. Standing on the scale and seeing the numbers go down, I couldn't keep from giggling. I just couldn't believe what was happening. I remember thinking, *If I keep going like this, someday I may actually weigh what it says on my driver's license!*

The sound of my laughter made me think of Sarah back there in Old Testament times, laughing when God told her she was going to get pregnant at the age of ninety. Her husband, Abraham, laughed too, after he fell flat on his face, apparently in shock. What a funny scene (see Genesis 17:17 and Genesis 18:11–13). Nine months later, they named their baby Isaac, which means laughter.

As I watched the numbers go down, I thought about naming my bathroom scale Isaac too. And believe me, that's *not* the name I would have given it in previous years!

By the time I had to leave for the next Women of Faith conference, I was eating soft foods like smoothies, oatmeal, and mashed potatoes. My mom went with me to the conference, just so I had someone along to help if any problems developed while I was traveling. I took along a supply of soups and instant oatmeal that I could heat and eat.

One of the most important concerns during this liquid and soft-diet stage is getting enough protein, so I nearly always carried some kind of protein drink with me. By the way, the Vivanno protein smoothies at Starbucks are delicious. And our dogs, Lucky and Pippin, who ride along every morning as I drive Sam to school and then stop by Starbucks on the way home, highly recommend the

Puppuchino, a little cup of whipped cream that Starbucks makes for its canine customers. It's an off-the-menu item you have to ask for, and Pippin says to tell you it's best with a swirl of vanilla. But I digress. . . .

Genesis 18:11 says Sarah laughed when God said she would get pregnant. I laughed when I stepped on the scale. Maybe Sarah and I were thinking, *Can this really be happening to me? ME? After all the things I've tried?*

When I got back with my Women of Faith team, they said all the right things, of course, asking how I felt and telling me I looked marvelous. I loved them all over again for their support, and although I probably didn't say it, I wanted to tell them, *Sisters, you ain't seen nuthin' yet!*

I had such confidence that I was on the right path, and no wonder! Look at the support system I had: God's love and strength empowering me in response to my faith that he would make everything work for good, plus the support of my family and friends, and the knowledge I needed to understand the process. Now I'd been given an additional gift, a surgical modification that would give me practical assistance in real life–out there where the rubber meets the road. Or maybe I should say, where the fork hits the plate.

As my kids might say, I was *pumped!*

JUMPING THE HURDLES

Off I went on this amazing new adventure. I'm writing this book about eighteen months after the surgery, and from this looking-back perspective, I can see mistakes and accidents, surprises and accomplishments. It's been quite a ride, getting up to and over this edge that's bringing me into a healthier life. There have been some challenges along the way, that's for sure!

For instance, during last year's long Christmas tour with my band, a rather violent round of stomach flu hit everyone on the bus during one challenging week of traveling together. You know the symptoms: fever, nausea, diarrhea, vomiting, and ultimately, an urge to crawl in a hole and die. It was *bad*. But in this business, the show must go on, or the paychecks don't come. So we kept going. No one missed a performance, and somehow we all survived it.

I suffered the episodes of vomiting just like everyone else. For a singer they're even worse because the stomach acid that's coming back up through the esophagus and over the vocal cords can affect the voice. I prayed and I rested, and by the time we rolled into Fort Worth for two concerts there, I had recovered, although I still wasn't eating or drinking much of anything.

For one thing, I still didn't feel like eating. For another, the vomiting had caused my stomach to become swollen around the Lap-Band site. So even when I did feel like eating or drinking, there was a chance the stuff wouldn't go down because the food passage was restricted by the swelling. I'd been told during the training and counseling sessions that this could happen, so I wasn't alarmed by it. I simply understood it was something I had to endure while my body recovered from the flu.

In Fort Worth, the concert hall was packed, and the first night's audience was wonderfully enthusiastic and responsive. We were rolling along through the show, and after one of the songs, I took a sip of water, as I often do to keep my throat moist and my voice working properly. We started the next song—I think it was "Go Tell It on the Mountain"—and after a few bars, I felt a disturbing sensation in my body.

Something isn't right.

I tried to focus on the song lyrics and managed to belt out a few more bars, but the sensation was intensifying. So determinedly was I focusing on the music that it took me a moment to realize exactly what was happening. Then it hit me: *Oh, my gosh! I'm gonna throw up!*

The sip of water I'd taken had apparently gone down my throat and hit the swollen area of stomach around the Lap-Band site, and now it was working its way back up my esophagus. In the middle of the song, I waved my hand toward the audience in what I hoped was an *I'll be right back* signal. Then I walked off the stage.

The guys in the band are 100 percent professional. They kept right on playing, jamming it up and filling in as though it were all part of the plan. But I'm sure they were thinking, *What the heck is happening?* Being the loyal friends they are, they knew me well enough to believe that, first, something *bad* must be happening but, second, somehow I'd be back because, yes indeed, the show must go on.

I headed for a tall trash can I saw in the backstage area, praying that what I thought was about to happen wouldn't. I stood by the trash can a moment, swallowing and trying to slow my breathing. It didn't take long for the sensation to pass. I didn't throw up, thank goodness. In just a few seconds I was back on stage.

I gave the band a little "cut" sign and then told the audience a little white lie, blaming the problem on hormones. "Menopausal women don't have hot flashes; we have power surges," I said. (I mean, I couldn't stand there and say, "I thought I was going to vomit"!) I finished up by joking, "Remember: *we* are professionals. Don't try this at home!" Then we went on with the rest of the show—without my taking any more sips of water in between the songs.

You know what they say about those dark clouds: each one has a silver lining. The good thing that came out of that little challenge was that at our next stop, in Wichita Falls, Texas, I got to meet a wonderful bariatric doctor who reinforced my high admiration for those who work in that specialty.

We rolled into Wichita Falls Saturday morning, where we would be performing at a big church that night. I asked the music minister of the church if he could help me make contact with a bariatric doctor who could adjust my Lap-Band to help me get through the current problem. The music minister knew exactly who to call.

This kind doctor, who wasn't a member of that church and had never heard of Sandi Patty, met me at his office on that Saturday evening. He removed a little water from the Lap-Band, something that's easily done through a port embedded under the skin, so that it would loosen up just a bit and help relieve my stomach's swelling at the site.

I had brought along some of my CDs and DVDs to give him as a thank you gift for seeing me on a Saturday. When we were all done, I asked how much I owed him.

"You don't owe me anything," he said. "It's my privilege to help you. I love seeing how happy patients are with their new lives after this procedure."

That's what I love about bariatric doctors: they love helping make their patients' dreams come true. They see people like me who come in on the edge of disaster, and a few months or a year later, they see us living an entirely different, healthy life.

Sometimes it all makes me think about the nursery rhyme describing ol' Humpty Dumpty sitting on the wall. He's up there teetering this way and that. Finally he falls, and look what happens.

But what if he'd fallen on the *other* side of the wall? Maybe there would have been wise and helpful people waiting there—not all the king's horses and all the king's men but folks who actually knew how to help him put his life back together again.

I think of it as Mr. Dumpty having a choice; that's what an edge is sometimes, a choice. We teeter on that edge, looking on either side of the wall. Neither landing site looks comfortable; there are rocks and sharp points to be endured. But sometimes, if you look a little farther in this imaginary scene, you can make a better choice by checking out the first responders waiting to pick up the pieces.

On one side, maybe you can see a hearse surrounded by a coroner's crew, or maybe a trash truck is waiting to haul you off to the landfill. "Off to the dump with you, Mr. Dumpty!"

On the other side you see a team of rescuers. Look: that's an ambulance waiting, with its motor running. And what's that painted on the top of the ambulance? Why, of course! It's a big red *cross*.

THE CONTINUING CHALLENGE
OF THE "INSIDE JOB"

Teetering up there on Humpty Dumpty's wall, I had a choice, and I chose to fall on the side where help was waiting for me. It still wasn't going to be easy or comfortable, but I wasn't going to rebuild my life alone.

Many of the challenges I've faced during that rebuilding work stem from the response I had during my first get-acquainted session with my "rescuers." During the first informational sessions about the Lap-Band, when I had realized that weight loss is an inside job, I'd seen that overeating is more about what's happening in my head than in my stomach.

But just because I know in my head what I should do, that doesn't mean I always do it. As the apostle Paul wrote, "What I don't understand about myself is that I decide one way, but then I act another, doing things I absolutely despise" (Romans 7:14).

One "despised" thing I'm trying not to give in to—with limited success—is my tendency to second-guess what others say to me. I tend to assume that hidden messages exist in others' words. After all, when the abusive teacher-babysitter stood me in the corner of her classroom she whispered to me that I *knew* what I had done wrong without her having to say it aloud. Her harsh accusation implied that not only had I done something wrong in the classroom, I'd also done something bad that resulted in her abusing me when I was left in her care.

If that teacher was communicating hidden messages, surely others were too, and somehow I was supposed to intuitively *know*.

Over the years, skillful therapists have helped me identify this destructive tendency, and they've also helped me work to overcome it. Most of the time, of course, the hidden messages I *assume* are being silently communicated are totally false. But that doesn't stop me from believing them. Usually the hidden messages are negative, hurtful, or disturbing.

For instance, when I leave home to keep some kind of performance date, whether it means I'll be away overnight or for a week or more at a time, Don says, "Have a good trip, honey. I'm going to miss you."

When I'm second-guessing what he really means, I mentally hear, *I wish you weren't leaving. I wish you were staying here. You're letting down our family by traveling so much. You should be more devoted to me and to our kids.*

Now, Don would never, ever say or even imply that kind of thing. I *know* that. But that doesn't keep me from struggling with "hearing" that kind of unspoken message again and again. I'm still battling that "despised" thing of second-guessing what's said to me.

The counseling sessions that prepared me for weight-loss surgery added another insightful lesson. I started seeing the ugly chain of events that happen when I feel hurt or anxious as a result of my second-guessing what people are saying to me. A "natural" way to respond might be to fire back a sharp reply to what I (mistakenly) assumed was a sharp message to me. But that's not what I did. I stuffed those feelings back inside, leaving them unsaid. And what did I use to do that stuffing? Food. I comforted myself by eating.

The good news is, I *am* making progress on one part of the problem. I no longer use food to stuff back the words I "want" to say in response to these unspoken (and most likely false) messages. But that opens up a whole new challenge, as you might imagine! Now, it sometimes seems that those cranky, wrongheaded remarks just come spurting out of my mouth, dumbfounding everyone within hearing range—including me! My family will tell you I've gotten quite a little 'tude going now and then, and they've been startled to hear me snap and snarl at them in ways I never did before.

One of my counselors compared it to an Oklahoma oil well. When the drill finally hits oil, the first stuff that comes up isn't the good, rich oil that's appreciated. It's the gunky, stinky, toxic stuff that no one wants.

Here's how that situation played out in a recent exchange between Don and me. I was out on the road last fall while our college-age children, Donnie and Aly, were moving into an apartment. During an otherwise ordinary phone call, I asked Don, "How are things going for them?"

"Well, they don't have any furniture, so probably the sooner we can help them with that situation, the better."

That's all Don said. But the second-guessing process immediately started in my head. The silent, hurtful message I thought I heard Don say was, *You're not working enough. We don't have enough money to buy them furniture. You're not doing your part.*

That kind of "accusation" hurt my feelings. In the past I might have stewed and fumed and eaten a package of cookies. But I'm no longer using food to stuff my feelings, so those feelings came spewing out of my mouth as words, catching Don totally off guard.

"Well, I'm out here working," I said coldly.

My dukes went up, and I instantly acted to defend myself—even though there had been no attack at all. There *was* no hidden message. Don was simply giving me an update on the kids' status.

I *know* that response was rooted way back there in that childhood abuse when I *didn't* think I could defend myself. But old habits die hard, and now I don't have my old friend Food to help me soothe the troubling feelings my second-guessing unleashes. Instead, without thinking, that day I responded to the unspoken message, determined to take the first punch.

But Don is on to me. I've shared with him how this whole ugly process works, and now he recognizes it when he hears or sees it. That day he answered simply, "Honey, did you call me to fight?"

Which was the best thing he could have said. He didn't jump in. He just reminded me, in a sweet, subtle way that I had fallen back into the old rut, but in a different and destructive way. With love and patience, he reached down to pull me out of it.

Of *course* I didn't call to fight. Of *course* Donnie and Aly need furniture. End of story!

A woman's intuition can be one of her strongest strengths: *something tells me he's not saying what he really means.* But I'm learning to recognize the situations when my God-given intuition is being overruled by the impulsive second-guessing that originated, not with God, but with that abusive babysitter so many years ago.

Every time I overcome that challenge, I move closer to the edge that separates my past life from the life God wants me to have today, one that's blessed by health and happiness.

RECOGNIZING THE VALUE OF CHALLENGES

There's value in challenges. For one thing, they can bring us closer to God. When we face some overwhelming problem or when we're urgently trying to overcome some despised thing, we cry out to him, begging him to help us. And in response, as the friend of Job told his problem-prone pal, "God always answers, one way or another, even when people don't recognize his presence" (Job 33:12).

The apostle Paul instructed us to "be cheerful no matter what; pray all the time; thank God *no matter what happens*"

(1 Thessalonians 5:16, italics added). We should be thankful for the problems we encounter because God may be using them to snap us out of whatever distractions we've drifted into. As Job's friend also said, God may use our difficulties to "get [our] attention through pain" (Job 33:19).

When God finally *gets* our attention, we're wise to keep it focused on him–because that's how we'll get through the next challenge, which is probably waiting right around the corner.

And through it all, we have to remember that no matter what kind of tangled-up mess we've landed in, God is going to use it for our ultimate good.

My musical director, Steve Potts, reminded me of that during another Christmas tour conversation among the band members. We were talking about the challenges and difficulties we've all faced, and Steve said thoughtfully, "Sometimes great things come from disasters."

"What do you mean?" I asked him.

"Well, Sandi, look what we're doing right now," he said. "We're on a concert tour that will include your performing with local symphonies in some of the cities. You started working with symphonies and doing more Broadway tunes and patriotic songs during that time after your divorce, when it looked like your career in Christian music was over. That's also when you started expanding into corporate concerts."

Steve was right. In the middle of all the devastating fallout over my inappropriate relationship with Don before my divorce was finalized, I still had a family to support. I needed to keep working, but churches and Christian radio shows had given up on me, so I had to look for other audiences. As a result of that challenge, my work with symphonies all around the country began.

It's been a wonderful thing for me, fun and rewarding work in a completely different setting than I had in the early days of my career. It includes the music of Broadway as well as pop tunes and songs from other eras. I started doing more concerts in corporate settings such as national and international trade and professional conferences. Now that many Christian organizations have forgiven and accepted me again, I'm blessed to have opportunities in a wider variety of venues than ever before, both Christian and secular. It wouldn't have happened without the tough challenges and hard lessons that pushed my career right up to that cliff-edge.

THE SHOW WITHIN THE SHOW

While I'm sharing some of the challenges I've faced as a performer, this might be a good place to take a little break and share some inside humor, just for fun. Sometimes when my band and I are up on stage, there's the show you see–and the show you don't see, as Stix says.

For example, one time we were performing a series of concerts in a city that was, quite frankly, too small for a *series* of concerts. *One* would have been plenty. Instead, we were there for several days, performing nightly, and the audiences were small and . . . well, they were polite, bless their hearts, but there just wasn't a lot of enthusiasm.

We did our best, and I hope the audience didn't notice, but the fact was, by the last show our energy was starting to drop, and we were all getting a little loopy. In between songs, I thought I heard one of the guys say quietly to himself, "Wow, they almost clapped for *that* one."

The show's program included Steve and me playing a wildly boisterous piano-duet interlude during one of the songs. I would sing the beginning lyrics and get the song going, and then I would walk over to the piano, sit down beside Steve on the bench, and we'd both pound away for a while before I got back up and returned to the microphone to sing the rest of the lyrics.

That night, I was wearing a brand-new dress for the first time. Thanks to my weight loss, I was starting to wear things that fit a little more snugly and showed off my emerging figure. When it was time for me to join Steve at the piano, I headed for the bench but then swerved and stood behind it, leaning over to reach the keys. I hope it looked to the audience like we were commending and encouraging each other or exclaiming what a great time we were having as we shouted back and forth, smiling widely while our fingers raced over the keys. But here's what we were *really* saying:

> Me: I can't sit down!
> Steve: Okay.

Then Steve gave the band a signal to speed things up.

> Me: (*screeching*): No! (I mean, I was already off
> balance, having to lean over the piano bench

          to reach the keys in my too-tight dress. And
          he wanted us to play *faster*?)
       Steve: (*scoldingly*): Watch your voice!

Then he gave the guys the signal to speed things up even *more*.

       Me: I'm telling you–you'll never work in this
          town again!
       Steve: *Promise?!*

We do have fun up there, at least when all our limbs and digestive organs are working properly. As we travel together, we love remembering stage-show adventures we've had. Recently we were laughing about a show we did out west several years ago as part of the entertainment for a huge gathering of a global corporation's employees. We were just one part of a multifaceted package; among the other entertainers were some cowboys who were to ride onto the stage on horseback and perform some rope tricks.

Due to flight delays, Steve wasn't able to get there in time for the regular rehearsals, but he did get there in time for what we call the tech rehearsal. We didn't even have time to brief him about the other parts of this amazing show. He just came hurrying in, sat down at the piano, and things immediately started.

Well, the poor horses weren't accustomed to walking on the slick stage floor, and there had already been some problems during the earlier rehearsals. Everyone but Steve knew that.

So the tech rehearsal began, and as the handlers were leading the horses into the backstage area, one of them slipped and fell. By that time we were performing one of our songs, but then someone came striding onto the stage yelling, "Horse down!"

Steve wasn't sure what he was supposed to do because he thought he'd misheard what was said.

"Excuse me?" he asked.

"Horse down!" the director yelled again.

"I'm having trouble understanding you," Steve said. "It almost sounded like you said, 'Horse down.'"

"That's what I said," the director barked: "Horse down!"

Poor Steve hadn't even known there were horses in the show. You know, it's just not something that's usually included in a Sandi Patty concert! So he was completely confused. Meanwhile pandemonium reigned backstage, out of Steve's sight, where the poor horse was floundering around, trying to regain its footing, and startling the other horses in the process.

For a few moments it seemed like the whole cast and crew dissolved into one grand discombobulation while Steve sat quietly at the piano, wondering what in the world was going on. The handlers finally put resin on the horses' hooves to give them some traction, and eventually, rehearsal resumed. The show came together later without any further calamities. But we're still laughing about the story many years later.

CHOOSING OUR CHALLENGES

There's a lot of laughter in show business, as well as risks and challenges. Sometimes, though, we can choose the risks and challenges we face, both in show business and in life. Some risks are daunting; others are done for fun. I'm thinking of the chapter of my life when my kids were participating in high school show-choir competitions.

You see, I've always been that one mom in the crowd who's so absorbed in the kids' performance that I'm sitting there in my seat, mouthing the words, singing along, and doing all the motions and actions right along with the choir.

And that's a problem. Not just because it embarrasses my kids to no end, but also because it's illegal. During one competition at Disney World I almost caused our show choir to get kicked out because the judges mistook my wild gyrations and lip-synch shadowing for *conducting*. And in the world of show-choir competitions, you are *not* allowed to conduct from the audience.

It was embarrassing to be called out for my behavior– and also extremely difficult to behave myself so that the kids could continue in the competition. Sitting there with my lips zipped and my hands and feet frozen in place was really, *really* hard!

And, please forgive me for digressing again, but may I just tell you that one of the biggest thrills of my past year was getting to meet the cast of the hit TV show *Glee*, which is the ongoing story of a high school show choir.

I shook hands with all of them and tried to offer a few

little tidbits of insight, coming from my perspective look-ing back. "Enjoy this journey," I told them. "Enjoy this season of your life, and remember that the people who loved you before all this started for you are still going to be there when all this fades. I know where you guys are right now. I hope you enjoy it—but also remember where you've come from."

Then the most amazing thing happened. The cast was practicing for a performance at an upcoming World Series game; they'd been invited to sing the national anthem. The young star who would be singing the melody wasn't able to be at the rehearsal, so guess who got to sing it with the awesome cast of *Glee* backing her up!

Not braggin'. Just sharin' my testimony.

FACING CHALLENGES
WITH THE RESCUER'S HELP

In this book I'm sharing my journey along and over the edge of the divine, a continuum that includes the profound as well as the trivial. Many times we have to work through challenges to get past the edge that separates us from the blessings God wants to give us. Amid those challenges, large or small, our best hope is to accept the aid of those ready-to-help rescuers waiting on the right side of Humpty Dumpty's wall.

For me, they're my friends and family and colleagues in the music world. But all of them work alongside the greatest Rescuer of us all. Since the dawn of time, he has stood ready to put the pieces of our lives back together again when we heed and accept the help he's offered us through so many voices.

The prophet's voice: "This is God's Message, the God who made earth, made it livable and lasting, known everywhere as *God:* 'Call to me and I will answer you. I'll tell you marvelous and wondrous things that you could never figure out on your own'" (Jeremiah 33:2).

The psalmist's voice: "He heals the heartbroken and bandages their wounds. . . . GOD puts the fallen on their feet again" (Psalm 147:2, 6).

Jesus' voice: "Are you tired? Worn out? Burned out on religion? Come to me. Get away with me and you'll recover your life. . . . Keep company with me and you'll learn to live freely and lightly" (Matthew 11:28, 30).

The apostle Paul's voice: "Don't fret or worry. Instead of worrying, pray. Let petitions and praises shape your worries into prayers, letting God know your concerns. Before you know it, a sense of God's wholeness, everything coming together for good, will come and settle you down. It's wonderful what happens when Christ displaces worry at the center of your life" (Philippians 4:6–7).

NOT THERE YET

I have to admit, I'm not there yet, not at that place where Christ completely displaces all the worry in my life. I do have moments—even days—of clarity and peace, but whenever I let my guard down, those demons of doubt and worry sneak back in, clouding my vision and stealing my resolve.

Maybe you're familiar with that edge of the divine too? If so, you know that it feels almost like we've been to the promised land and then backtracked again. We've crossed that edge, passed through the Jordan in triumph; but then something happens, and the next thing we know, we're back on the other side.

Back in the wilderness. And boy, does *that* place feel familiar.

SEVEN

Choose Life!

I place before you Life and Death,
Blessing and Curse. Choose life.

—Deuteronomy 30:19

In the thirtieth chapter of Deuteronomy, God is patiently explaining the choices available to the Israelites as they consider the future available to them in the promised land. As I read the words of that powerful chapter, I tend to see God wearing a white coat, standing at the head of a long conference table in a bariatric surgeon's office. He's describing what life could be like for me on both sides of the edge I'm teetering on. Here are some of the highlights of his words to the Israelites–and to me:

> You will make a new start, listening obediently to God, keeping all his commandments that I'm commanding you today. GOD, your God, will outdo himself in making things go well for you. . . . But only if you listen obediently to GOD, your God, and keep the commandments and regulations. . . . This commandment that I'm commanding you today isn't too much for you, it's not out of your reach. . . . The word is right here and now–as near as the tongue in your mouth, as near as the heart in your chest. Just do it!

Look at what I've done for you today: I've placed in
front of you
> Life and Good
> Death and Evil.

And I command you today: Love GOD, your God.
Walk in his ways. Keep his commandments, regula-
tions, and rules so that you will live, really live, live
exuberantly, blessed by GOD, your God, in the land you
are about to enter and possess.

But I warn you: If you have a change of heart,
refuse to listen obediently, and willfully go off to serve
and worship other gods, you will most certainly die.
You won't last long in the land that you are crossing
the Jordan to enter and possess. (selected passages
from Deuteronomy 30, verses 8–18)

God continues to offer us that same choice every day
of our lives. When we're feeling arrogant and wise, we
think, *Duh! Who wouldn't know which side of that edge to
choose?*

Yet, like the Israelites, we wander away, get distracted, let ourselves be lured off into the wilderness by
other gods. When one of our "other gods" is food, we
battle continual temptation, and sometimes we yield to
it. Not because we don't know better but because we're
human.

Earlier I mentioned the altar God directed the Israelites
to build out of stones they had picked up out of the Jordan

as they crossed it to enter the promised land. He told them the altar would be a reminder of his faithfulness to them. When their children asked why the altar was there, he said, tell them the amazing story of "how strong GOD's rescuing hand" had been in bringing them to the land of milk and honey (see Joshua 4:24).

But when I think of that altar, standing on the banks of the Jordan, I have to wonder, *Was it built there to serve as a reminder in another way too?* Was it meant to serve as a reminder to those who were crossing the Jordan a second time, or a third time, or a tenth? Maybe they had felt the pull of those other gods, calling from back over there on the other side, calling from the wilderness, and even though they knew better, maybe they did the despised thing. Maybe some of them ended up back in the wilderness.

As I imagine it, I'm one of them. I've been tempted by one of those other, despised gods, and I'm back in the wilderness, but I wake up and think, *Dear God, what have I done? Please, Father, can you forgive me? Can you give me another chance?*

"Sure, honey," God says. "You just swim across the Jordan again, and come on home."

And that's what I do. Then, as I drag my weak and exhausted self up the bank on the far side of the Jordan, I see it, that altar. It reminds me all over again that, no matter what, God is faithful. He has promised, "'Even if the mountains walk away and the hills fall to pieces, My love won't walk away from you, my covenant commitment of peace won't fall apart.' The God who has compassion on you says so" (Isaiah 54:9).

My dear friend Carolyn Gill, who also happens to be a fantastic life coach, recommended that I carry a heavy rock around with me to remind myself of the senseless worries and problems I burden myself with needlessly. The rock would represent all the stupid decisions and bad choices I've made.

"You carry that thing around, Sandi, and let it remind you of what you already know," she said. "You'll quickly see that it's too heavy to carry; hauling it around is too exhausting. Then remember that you can *choose* to set it down, let it go. You don't have to carry it around with you."

Actually, I can see my boulder of burdens having another therapeutic purpose as well. I can imagine the rock being one I pulled from the Jordan as I crossed into the land of God's promises the first time. It could remind me of his faithfulness throughout my own amazing story.

And then, when that rock grows heavy enough to stop me, maybe I'll finally realize that Carolyn is right and I don't have to carry it around with me. As a matter of fact, I can think of the ideal place to put that burden of worries and problems: right there at the image of another extraordinary altar.

The cross where Jesus died.

That's where we leave the sins and burdens he died to save us from. That's where God revealed his ultimate vow to us of forever-faithfulness.

HARD CHOICES, SOFT LANDINGS

Back when I was in the turbulent season of my life, suffering the consequences of the poor choices I'd made and looking for a way out of the mess I'd landed in, I had a strong and enlightening dream. I can close my eyes even now and remember it as vividly as I did when I woke up from it all those years ago.

In the dream, I'm clinging to the limb of a scrawny little tree that's growing out of the very edge of a cliff. All around me a storm is raging, and the powerful wind is blowing me away from the cliff and out over the abyss. Far below I can see the sharp rocks that will undoubtedly end my life. All that's saving me is my death grip on the branch of that little tree, and I can feel myself growing weaker by the second. I can't hang on much longer.

Suddenly, above the howling roar of the wind, I hear a voice, and instantly I recognize it as God's.

Let go, God says.

In the dream, I close my eyes. I can't bear to look at the murderous rocks any longer.

Let go, God says again.

My life is almost over. The only thing I have left is a choice. That's all. I can choose to let the wind do whatever it will with me, blow me over the edge whenever it wants to. Or I can *choose* to let go. I can *choose* to follow God's voice *now*.

That's what I do. I choose to let go, and down I fall.

But, unknown to me, the wind has changed. It's blowing

the other way, no doubt in obedience to the voice who stilled it completely one stormy night on the Sea of Galilee two thousand years ago (see Matthew 8:23–27).

In my dream, the wind has changed direction, and when I choose to heed God's voice and let go of the tree limb, I fall onto solid ground.

We have choices as we balance precariously on the edge of the divine. We can choose to put our faith in God and make good choices in obedience to his will. Or we can make the other choice and head for the abyss.

Every day I ask God to help me make wise choices that keep me close to his heart and his will. In so many ways, I see the rewards of those decisions.

Let me just say, before we go on, how blessed I've been and how thankful I am that throughout my life I've been surrounded by special people, including friends who have chosen to support me with their love and prayers–and laughter. Two of those friends, Gene and Geri Anderson, live in South Carolina. Gene is now slowed by Parkinson's disease, so we don't get to see each other as much as we'd like. But when last year's Christmas tour rolled through their hometown, we got to visit a little while.

I was telling them about the book I was writing, *The Edge of the Divine*, which would talk about the edges we encounter in our lives, those points where something is likely to begin. We talked about choices that arise as we travel along those edges, and Gene immediately thought of a joke. It reminds me of my dream, but it has a funny–and insightful–twist:

A man is walking on a cliff, and all of a sudden, he trips and slips over the edge. As he falls he manages to grab a pitiful little tree root sticking out of the cliff. The root isn't strong enough to hold him for long, and the man frantically calls for help. He screams and yells until his voice is almost gone. "Help! Help! Is anyone up there?"

"Yes," says a voice from above. "I'm here."

"Thank heaven! Can you help me?" the man asks desperately.

"Yes," the voice says again. "I can help you."

"Oh, thank you! Thank you for helping me," the man says. Then he asks, "Who are you?"

"I'm God," the voice answers.

"God! Oh, thank you, God! What do you want me to do?"

"Let go," God tells him.

"What?" the man asks, looking down at the ugly rocks hundreds of feet below.

"Let go," God says again.

The man is silent a moment. Then he looks upward and asks, "Is anyone else up there?"

A New Beginning

Some of the choices we encounter along the cliff-edge seem awfully scary, don't they? When we're at the point where something is likely to begin, it usually means something else is likely to end, depending on the choice we make.

Even though the new thing looks appealing, that old thing can seem safer, less risky, more comfortable. And sometimes our choices impact others in ways we don't expect.

My husband is gifted in connectedness. He is constantly thinking of ways to draw his loved ones close to his heart, so it just follows that he and God have a very close-knit relationship. Don loves God with every ounce of his being, and he demonstrates it in the choices he makes.

For several years, he worked in the Character Counts program at Anderson University, and he helped expand the program to one that gained widespread recognition as an essential component of AU students' college experience and as a model for how character development can be incorporated into a curriculum.

In 2008, he had organized a big conference at the university that would draw participants from a wide area of the country. And then, after he'd put hours and hours of effort into planning the event, it had to be canceled for reasons beyond Don's control. He was *so* disappointed.

But while organizing the event, and also through other work he'd done related to Character Counts, he had made some valuable contacts. And just as he was sadly sending out the notices that the conference was being canceled, he got a call from one of those corporate contacts asking about ways to help fund the job Don was already doing in Character Counts.

During the summer, Don continued to talk to this company, Sandridge Energy, which is based in Oklahoma City. And then—well, let me just say it the way *I* tell the story; Don would never say this: the more the folks in the Oklahoma City company worked with Don, the more they fell in love with him. Which just shows you what an excellent judge of character this outfit is!

Don kept me updated on what was going on, and he'd also mentioned the company to the kids, letting them know about the support he was getting. It became obvious that he was enjoying working with the people at the company as much as they were liking what they saw in him.

Then some kind of turning point occurred, some kind of edge was crossed, and in the fall, the Oklahoma people offered Don a job—a position they would be creating just for him, one he could shape and develop into a character-education program, designed specifically for Sandridge Energy, to enhance its relationship and outreach to the community.

Don told me about it, and I didn't even blink. "That's awesome!" I told him. "Let's go! You've gotta do it."

"Really?" he asked. "Even if it means leaving Anderson? I mean, the kids have grown up here, our home is here, everybody's *here*."

"But most of them are grown now; Anna's married and five are in college," I answered. "Sam's so adaptable, I know he'll be happy wherever we land. Mollie's probably the one it'll matter most to because she'll be a senior next year, but we can work something out for her."

Next Don shared the news with our kids when everyone was home for dinner one night. They all agreed it sounded like a perfect opportunity for him.

"Even if it means moving to Oklahoma?" he asked them, just as he had asked me.

"Sure, Dad," everyone said.

The school year had begun. Sam was starting middle school; Mollie was a junior in high school. Donnie, Aly, Erin, Jenn, and Jonathan were living in apartments while they continued their studies at Anderson University. Anna and her husband, Collin, lived thirty minutes away in Indianapolis.

Later that fall, the Oklahoma City company made Don an official job offer.

"Are you sure about this, Sandi?" Don asked me. "You're really okay with moving to Oklahoma City? You think it'll be okay for our family?"

"Absolutely!" I answered. "Don, six of our kids are already out on their own. You know, kids leave home; that's the way life is supposed to be. Now that they're adults and living on their own, we're freer to make the moves *we* need to make. It'll be fine. Let's go!"

I knew how hard Don had worked to get to that moment. He'd always put his family first, staying in Anderson when he probably could have gotten better-paying, more rewarding jobs elsewhere. A few years earlier, he'd worked extra hard to complete an advanced degree. He had great experience, great skills, and wisdom. He was so capable. He'd enjoyed his work at Anderson University, but we all knew he was qualified, primed, and ready for bigger opportunities. That was exactly what the Oklahoma company was offering him: a choice to use his abilities in an exciting new way.

"Don, say yes," I told him. "This is the opportunity of a lifetime."

At another family get-together, we told the kids the news. Congratulations and good luck wishes filled the room.

The plan was that Don would move to Oklahoma City in January. I'd stay behind in Anderson so that Sam and Mollie could finish out the semester, and then we'd join him in late spring, when school was out. Again, everyone expressed support and enthusiasm.

We had a wonderful Christmas together, even though it was a little poignant because we knew Don would be leaving soon, and we knew it was the last Christmas we'd spend together in that big, beautiful house we'd lived in for more than ten years. It has a large bay window that overlooks a long Indiana cornfield. As always, we put a huge Christmas tree in that window with piles of presents all around. As always, we gathered at the large table we'd had custom built to accommodate all of us in the breakfast nook. As always, we talked and ate and laughed a lot. It was a warm and love-filled time.

Then, as the days rolled by and Don's departure grew nearer, I was surprised to sense an unsettling feeling of dread growing steadily in my heart. We'd spent so much time apart, with my need to be on the road so frequently, that I hadn't expected that Don's moving to Oklahoma ahead of Sam, Mollie, and me would feel like a big deal. But, increasingly, it did.

The more I thought about the new chapter opening in his life, the more I wanted to be part of its beginning. I wanted to be there that first day when he came home from his new job and shared how it felt to have his dream come true. I wanted to be the one he told it all to.

Finally, a couple of days before his departure, I shared my feelings with Don. "I want to come with you," I told him.

A Sudden Good-bye

Arrangements were made, and plans were changed. Sam and I would move on out to Oklahoma City with Don. Mollie and Don's dad–our beloved Pop, who was living with us at the time–would stay behind in the Anderson house so Mollie could finish her junior year in the high school there. Anna and Collin and the five college kids were already settled in their own places, so they wouldn't be impacted any differently than they were before our plans suddenly changed.

I sent out a quick e-mail to let everyone know what was happening. There just wasn't time to make all those individual phone calls and rehash the whole change-in-plans thing again and again. An e-mail let me tell everyone the same thing at the same time. Thank goodness for modern technology!

We hurriedly packed all the clothes we'd need. We weren't taking furniture or household goods because we didn't have a house yet in Oklahoma. We would be spending our first few weeks in the home of our longtime friends (and former nanny) Betty Fair and her husband, Phil.

To me, it didn't feel all that different from packing up for a long weekend to work with Women of Faith or for a monthlong concert tour on the bus. I'd left home and had said good-bye to Don and the kids so many times over the years. This time I think I was actually glad to be leaving *with* Don and Sam, for a change.

Jonathan was at the house the morning we left. How appropriate, I thought, that he was there to see us off on this new chapter of our lives. Jonathan is one of my twins, and he had quite an adventure himself when he was just a toddler. A tall, heavy, old-fashioned coat tree fell on him, and one of the iron prongs fractured his skull. Some of his brain tissue was irreparably damaged and had to be removed.

When it happened, no one knew what Jonathan's future held. Doctors warned us that the brain damage could cause learning disabilities, and sure enough, Jonathan has had to work extra hard all his life to accomplish what might have been easy if the accident hadn't happened. His teachers told us not to think of learning *disabilities* but about the fact that Jonathan learns *differently*.

Now, twenty years later, Jonathan has excelled beyond anyone's dreams and is on his way to a full and productive life. In fact, soon after this book is published, Jonathan will be graduating from college. Yes, he's had to work harder than the other kids to get where he is academically. On the other hand, he has extraordinary musical gifts, and he especially loves movie scores and the way they help tell the story depicted on screen.

So, with that background, picture our little group,

Jonathan, Sam, Don, and me, standing in the driveway of our Anderson home on that cold January day. Our two cars were packed so full it was nearly impossible to see out the windows. Sam was riding with me, and just as we were leaving, Jonathan handed me two CDs.

"Mom, put this one in the CD player and push PLAY at the end of the driveway," he said, pointing to the first disk.

I pulled my tall, handsome son into my arms one more time, knowing he'd created something special. "Thank you, Jonathan."

I slipped into the driver's seat, closed the car door, turned the key, and slid the CD into the player. At the end of the driveway, I turned and looked back. Jonathan, standing in the driveway, waved good-bye. I pushed the PLAY button.

MUSICAL MEMORIES, MAGICAL MOMENTS

As I drove away from the Anderson house, the music on Jonathan's CD started softly and somberly as I left our neighborhood. It continued in a poignant, reflective key as I rolled by the street my parents live on, the road that goes to Sam's school, the turn we make to go to our church.

It picked up energy but kept its serious mood as I went past the street I'd come down to bring my babies home from the hospital. The music was sweet and introspective, perfectly matching my thoughts as I drove the familiar route out to the interstate. Jonathan had known what streets I would take, and he had put together segments of movie scores to create a haunting overture that perfectly reflected my emotions.

It was almost as if he knew which way my head would turn, which things I would see and remember as I made my way out of the city where we'd lived all these years–Jonathan's entire life. He had driven the route he knew I would take, timing his selections perfectly to create a sound track that would accompany me on my way.

It was amazing, but the best part was still ahead. As I veered onto the ramp leading up to the freeway, the music changed. The somber tone and minor key melded into a sweeping, uplifting swirl of excitement. The strings began a glorious chromatic scale that ascended into an eruption of celebration. The mood changed, and the horns joined in until the music became a grand, orchestral theme, joyous and victorious as I merged into the traffic on the interstate.

I felt as though I'd crossed an edge separating a poignant good-bye and a happy hello. I picked up speed, and the music swept me along. Jonathan had perfectly arranged and timed the songs to match what was happening in my heart as I rolled out of Anderson and into a new adventure, a new beginning.

HEADED WEST

Our little two-car caravan rolled across the Midwest as we opened that new chapter of our lives. I was born in Oklahoma, and both my parents grew up there. I was looking forward to reconnecting with my roots. My family had moved away when I was just a toddler, but facts are facts: I am a native Oklahoman.

We deliberately stopped in Sapulpa, my dad's hometown, and called him from a gas station. He told us, "I can picture right where you are."

At each Oklahoma stop, I understood a little better why my dad is the way he is: warm and conversational, one of those people who, as they say, doesn't know a stranger. He'll joke with people he's never met like they're friends he's known all his life.

For example, as we were walking into a restaurant, a couple about my parents' age were walking out.

"You're too late," the man told us with a pronounced Oklahoma twang. A toothpick protruded from the corner of his smile. "We already ate everything."

I had to laugh; I could absolutely hear my dad saying those same words.

A short while later, we rolled into Oklahoma City. I pointed out the tall building where Don would work. But Sam, being my son, seemed totally absorbed in noticing all the good restaurants the city had to offer. Then, as we turned off on our exit, there was our favorite, Braum's. Surely there could be no better omen.

We arrived at Phil and Betty Fair's house and celebrated the renewing of our long, heart-to-heart relationship. The next morning, I kissed Don good-bye as he left for his new job, already loving my new role as executive wife. Throughout our friendship and our marriage, Don has been my wingman. We met when he was one of my backup singers during the early days of my career, and he's always adapted *his* career to what was best for *my* circumstances. Now it was his turn to step into the spotlight and my turn to adjust, which I was happy to do.

During the drive from Indiana to Oklahoma, as I followed him down the interstate, a powerful Bible passage had come continually to mind. I'd learned Ruth's words to her mother-in-law Naomi as a child memorizing the verses from the King James version, and that's the way they kept replaying in my head and my heart: "Whither thou goest, I will go; and where thou lodgest, I will lodge: thy people shall be my people, and thy God my God" (Ruth 1:16).

The fact was, I just loved being Mrs. Don Peslis, and finally I was getting a chance to show it.

JUST THE RIGHT PLACE

The next thing on the to-do list was finding a house for us. I began working with a Realtor, and we must have looked at fifty houses. Seriously!

My routine became driving Sam to school with Betty each morning and then meeting the Realtor at Starbucks and spending the next few hours looking at houses. We wanted to stay in Phil and Betty's general area and school district, and we had agreed on a price range and a size—three bedrooms.

It seemed like a simple set of wishes, but we looked and

looked and looked and couldn't find just the right place. A couple of weeks went by, then another. It felt like we'd looked at every single house in the area, and nothing seemed to work. While Phil and Betty would never even hint that they were getting tired of having full-time houseguests, I knew how *I* would feel in their situation, and I knew we needed to be moving on. But where would we move *to*?

I've steadfastly stuck with my fitness plan since the Lap-Band surgery, and one of the first things I did was measure out a route in Phil and Betty's neighborhood so I knew the distance I would be covering on my daily walks. I walked that route so many times I knew every house–especially every house for sale–by heart.

One morning during my prayer time, I poured out my feelings to God. "Lord, I know you have the right house for us. *You* know you have the right house for us. Can you just tell us? Can you just guide our steps? Literally, God, I ask you to guide our steps as we move throughout each day. Help us find that house you have for us. And, Lord, for Betty and Phil's sake, please hurry."

Later that morning, I tied on my sneakers and set out on my walk. But inexplicably that day I set off in an entirely different direction. I didn't walk my usual route, the one I'd measured out so carefully and knew so well. I walked in a completely different direction.

Off I went, one step after another, until I got to the opposite end of Phil and Betty's housing development, an area I'd never walked in before. I passed by a house–I'm sure I had to have *driven* by it before, but somehow I'd never noticed it. And there it was, a FOR SALE sign in the yard. Hmm. Three bedrooms, a small yard, in exactly the neighborhood we loved. I hurried back to Betty's house and called the Realtor, asking her to e-mail me the details on the house I'd seen. As I read over them, one word came to mind.

Perfect.

Here's what I love about God's sense of humor. I hadn't said, "Lord, guide our *path*" or "*Direct* us the right way." I had said, "Guide our *steps*," and, wouldn't you know? I *walked* right by the house we ended up getting.

We had arrived in Oklahoma on January 12, 2008, and we moved into our new house on February 9. Because the house was new and empty, we could close the deal and move right in. Amazing, right? You would almost think it was the house God had meant for us to have.

Everything seemed to be falling into place as we happily settled into our new home. Although Sam missed his Indiana pals, he was enjoying his new school and making lots of friends, who instantly recognized him as a smart boy and cool guy. At least that's the way *I* observed the situation.

Just consider one of Sam's conversations with one of his new friends who said, "Sam, how do you get along so well with the girls? You always know just what to say to them. What makes the girls like talking with you? How do you do it?"

Sam smiled at his buddy and shook his head. "Dude," he said. "I have *five* sisters! I've learned that you just have to talk to girls like they're *normal people*."

AN UNEXPECTED UPSET

We missed Sam's five sisters, all living back in Indiana along with his two brothers, one brother-in-law, and three grandparents. But we honestly thought everything was going well. We had settled into our new life in Oklahoma and couldn't have been happier. Meanwhile, back in Indiana, we'd unknowingly created a hard situation for the kids we'd left behind.

We know *now* that our move wasn't as easy for them as any of us had anticipated. Sure, they're young adults, and yes, they're out there living on their own, for the most part, with financial help from us. They're smart and capable and creative. To Don and me, it simply felt like our kids had flown the nest, and now we were moving on to the next season of our lives.

But to the kids, it felt like their "nest" had been yanked out from under them, and now they had no place to land as they fluttered through the fast pace of college and music and busy social lives.

My oldest child, Anna, said it felt like they all lived in a snow globe. It had been shaken many times, but there was always a beautiful place for the "snowflakes" to land. Now it felt like that foundation had been taken away and they were left to aimlessly float around, trying to find the place that had disappeared.

"All of us kids have been through so much together," she said. "We've known each other since before our parents' divorces from their first husband and wife. When Mom and

Don married, we combined all of us into one big house, and that became our center. Over the years, we've been through a lot of things that are harder than moving—like when Donnie and Mollie and Aly's mom died—but the move to Oklahoma shook us more than almost anything else. Maybe because we've worked hard to stay connected emotionally and spiritually. But most of our memories of that connecting work seemed to be focused on the house we all shared. And also, it was more than the house. It was that Mom and Don were there, *in* the house. *They* are our family's center, even more than the house itself. It felt like suddenly they were gone."

Yes, the kids could still talk to us any time of the day or night on our cell phones. Yes, Nana and Papa and Pop were all still there, along with my kids' dad, and they were all ready to talk or tend to any of the kids in any way needed. But no longer could Anna, Collin, Jonathan, Jenn, Donnie, Aly, or Mollie pop by the house to share a moment with Don or me whenever feelings were hurt or classes seemed overwhelming or a hard decision had to be made. It just wasn't the same.

As one of them told us later, sure, kids leave home and go to college. But then it's *their* choice to leave. Don and I had moved away, and although we'd perfunctorily asked their opinion, I think they sensed that they actually had no choice in the matter at all.

It gradually became apparent to Don and me that we had some work to do back in Indiana. We needed to help our adult kids feel closure about what was happening. And, what a surprise! It turns out that a mom sending her kids an e-mail telling them she's moving across the country in a couple of days *isn't* the best way for her to let them know she's leaving them!

Anna said that, yes, they'd all agreed that Don should take the new job. And yes, they were all thrilled to understand what a grand new opportunity this meant for him. "We just hadn't really thought through what it meant for *us*," she said. "Of course we still wanted it to happen for Don. We just needed some help feeling reassured that we are all still connected as a family; we needed a little more attention than Mom and Don realized we needed."

The edge that had separated two happy chapters of my own life turned out to be a very hard edge for our children. We shared apologies, talked through issues, engaged counselors, and made some changes.

Not all of those changes made things easier for the kids, but at least this time we took time to explain to them what was happening. One change was that Don decided it was time to bring Mollie on out to Oklahoma ahead of the original plan, and that was a very hard change for her. She didn't like it one bit at the time and was quite angry at us.

Mollie had endured so much loss in her life, beginning with Don and her mother's divorce and then her mother's death due to cancer. She had lived with her mother in Michigan quite a while to help care for her sweet little sister Sidney after her mom remarried, and then, after her mother's death, she'd had to leave her Michigan friends to move back to Anderson to live with us. Now we were forcing her to leave *those* friends as well as her siblings to move yet again. She had every reason to be upset.

I'll never forget that long, painfully quiet drive from Indiana to Oklahoma when we brought her west to live with us. It was excruciating for all of us, but I agreed with Don that the four of us still living at home–Don and me plus Sam and Mollie–truly needed to be together.

When we pulled up to the new house in Oklahoma City, we gave Mollie a quick tour of the house, and then we showed Mollie her bedroom. She promptly stepped into the empty closet, closed the door, and sat down and cried.

It was a heartbreaking time for all of us. To see your child in pain is hard; to recognize that you, the parents, are the cause of the pain is paralyzing. We told Mollie, "You don't have to love it here, or even like it; you just have to show up every day. We understand this is hard for you, and that's all we're asking of you right now."

And that's what Mollie did. Some days there were tears, some days fears, some days anger. But every day she "showed up," staying engaged with her family and her new school. She kept putting one foot in front of the other until she got through that day . . . and then the month . . . and then the year. Seeing her keep going, even when it was so hard, my heart nearly burst with pride and admiration. She is a wonderfully strong young woman.

Meanwhile, Pop moved on to spend some time with one of his other sons, and we donated the use of the Anderson house to our church for an associate pastor and his wife and their seven children to live in for the rest of the year. It was a perfect fit for them, and after the time of donated rent ended, they decided to buy the house. So, in the end, the move was repeatedly confirmed to us as the right thing to do.

We all learned from it. Certainly Don and I learned that we are still a very important part of our older children's lives, even though they're adults now. I guess that surprises us a little bit, but it certainly pleases us too. And the kids learned a lot as well.

For one thing, they've learned to be more *intentional* about their relationship. They see that being connected now requires more than just happening to stop by and say hello or bumping into each other on campus or waving hello from one church pew to another. Now we all have to deliberately work at staying connected to each other, and I love the way that continues to happen for us.

Now, nearly two years later, Mollie, being the tough and creative young woman she is, has had a complete turn-around in her attitude about the move. If she ever takes one of those personality tests, I'll bet her therapist will see a lot of resilience in her responses too. One day recently, something pretty amazing happened. She told Don and me, "I just *love* Oklahoma City." Then she flashed her bright smile and said, "And you can Twitter that if you want."

Don and I looked at each other—and promptly passed out.

FAMILY MIGRATION

During the summer of 2009, Donnie and Jonathan came out to Oklahoma to spend the summer, and both of them

loved it. Afterward, Jonathan went back to Anderson to finish up at Anderson University, but Donnie decided to enroll
in the Academy of Contemporary Music at the University
of Central Oklahoma. It's a fabulous program, nicknamed
the School of Rock, developed in collaboration with the
Academy of Contemporary Music of London. His sister Aly
joined him, and what do you know? Now half of our kids–
Sam, Donnie, Mollie, and Aly–are living in Oklahoma. Sam
and Mollie are at home with Don and me while Donnie and
Aly are living in an apartment with some School of Rock
classmates.

It amazes me that, so far, all of our college kids have
chosen to study music in one form or another.

We're still working through some of the issues related
to our move to Oklahoma, but over all, I think we've crossed
the hardest edges into a divine world of greater family support and understanding. Along the way, there's been a lot of
stress and a lot of anxiety. It was hard to realize how much
we'd hurt our family, not really by what we'd done but by
the abrupt way we'd done it, at least in their eyes. As someone said, a mother is only as happy as her saddest child.
And I had a lot of sad children there for a while.

But they weren't so sad that they were sitting around
moping all the time, so desperate to see Mom and Dad again
that they were unable to function. At one point, Don and I
drove back to Indiana with Sam, Mollie, Donnie, and Aly
for a visit–just in time for Jenn, Erin, Jonathan, Anna, and
Collin to be off doing other things. Jenn was in California,
working with the Women of Faith Revolve tour, Jonathan

was visiting his girlfriend's family in Michigan, Erin had gone to Chicago with a friend, and Anna and Collin were away attending two different weddings. Then Donnie, Aly, and Mollie went on to Michigan to visit relatives there. Sam stayed busy visiting his Indiana friends. Which left Don and me sitting there in Anderson, wondering where everybody had gone and pondering what a strange little family we are.

When we got back to Oklahoma, the tempo of our lives seemed to speed up even more. There was just too much going on to keep track of. I was traveling nearly every weekend with Women of Faith. Sam and Mollie were busy with school activities and often needed transportation from one event to the next. Donnie and Aly were still settling into their apartment and adjusting to the new requirements at the School of Rock. Our house in Indiana had sold and had to be cleaned out.

It was all happening at once, and my old method of handling stress was now off limits to me. I couldn't soothe my anxiety by eating a dozen cookies anymore. I couldn't stuff down my feelings with an extra-large serving of ice cream. So sometimes those feelings came rushing out of my mouth like the snarls and snaps of a rabid dog–which caused the target of my remarks to feel just as upset as I did. And what did *that* accomplish?

Everybody needed my help or attention or time. And somehow in all the hubbub, I seemed to have slipped back across the Jordan. Without meaning to or realizing it had happened, I found myself back in a dark place, far from the promised land. Back in the wilderness.

I felt like I was hanging "on the cliff-edge of death, knowing the next breath may be [my] last" (Job 33:19). That's how the emergency room felt to me when I ended up there about a year after the Lap-Band surgery.

EIGHT

Enough

My grace is enough; it's all you need.
My strength comes into its own in your weakness.

–2 CORINTHIANS 12:7

It had been a busy day—and the day wasn't over yet. We'd been running around all over the place, getting kids settled in their apartment, talking with kids back in Indiana, making arrangements for different people to do different things, seeming to rush from one little "Mom, could you . . . ?" to the next. But at least we were home now, and the day's busyness seemed to be winding down.

I had felt a little "off" all day. At that point, I'd dropped about sixty pounds and was more active than I'd been since my teenage years. Most of the time I felt energetic and happy, but that day, a touch of nausea seemed to hover around whatever I was doing. It would threaten and then pass and then threaten again. A wave of clamminess would dampen my brow and then subside, only to recur an hour or so later. I kept going, though, hoping I wasn't coming down with something at the peak of the Peslis family's busiest season.

Then, as the sun was setting, the symptoms got worse. I felt lightheaded and couldn't seem to take a good, deep breath. My chest burned, and a giant hand seemed to be squeezing my ribcage.

I didn't want to alarm Don, Sam, and Mollie, but when I put all the symptoms together in my head, I thought I might be having a heart attack, and the mere thought of it made me feel panicky. *I don't have time for this!* I remember thinking—which only served to intensify all the other symptoms. I hated to alarm everyone, but I knew I was in trouble.

"Don, I just don't feel good," I told him quietly. "Would you mind driving me to the hospital? Whatever this is, I want to get on top of it early so I don't have to miss work later this week."

He'd known I wasn't feeling well, and he took one look at my ashen face and instantly stopped what he was doing and helped me toward the door. We were in the garage, getting into the car, when I passed out. Terrified, the kids called 911, and within minutes I was racing across town in an ambulance—with Don and the kids in hot pursuit.

We were in the emergency room several hours while all the tests were run. Lying there, letting myself be stuck, scanned, scoped, and monitored, I felt a strange swing of conflicting feelings. I'd worked so hard to lose weight, exercise, and get myself back to good health, and now look what had happened. I'd apparently done something terribly wrong. After all, healthy people don't spend the night in an emergency room being stuck, scanned, scoped, and monitored. *What a loser*, I thought. *What an embarrassment I must be to my family.*

A lot of strange thoughts can flash through your mind when you've lost all dignity and had all your most private body parts displayed to and handled by strangers.

I was lying there regretting all the inconvenience I was causing my family and worrying about how many Women of Faith dates I'd have to miss when the doctor came in with my test results. "Your heart is fine," he said. "Actually, it's in excellent condition."

I couldn't think of anything to say. Tears welled up in my eyes and, one by one, rolled over the edge and down my cheeks. I don't know whether I was crying from relief or humiliation. *I put my family through all this—and for nothing?*

The doctor went through the checklist, naming the tests and citing the results. Everything looked good.

The news was getting better. So why was I feeling worse?

"An anxiety attack can mimic all the symptoms of a heart attack," he told me. "You were right to come in and get checked out. Given how you were feeling, you could have been having a heart attack. But you weren't, and that's good news, isn't it?"

My tears didn't show signs of stopping anytime soon.

The doctor smiled, tilted his head, and asked in a friendly way, "Would there be any circumstances in your life that might be causing you extra amounts of stress right now?"

Finally, just what I needed: a joke!

"How much time you got?" I asked him, laughing as I wiped a tear dripping off my chin. Then I told him, "There just doesn't seem to be enough of me to go around."

It was an odd thing for me to say, wasn't it? I don't

really know why those specific words came out of my mouth, but as they did, something clicked inside my head, and another strange set of conflicting thoughts occurred to me. Physically there *was* much less of me to go around–sixty pounds less. Could it be that perhaps my smaller size was some kind of embodiment of the subconscious idea that, yes, I am superwoman and I can do all things–but now there's less of me, so I'm not quite as super as I used to be?

And yet, in contrast to that thought was the absolute confidence that I had never felt stronger, surer, and *larger*, somehow, more capable than ever before.

It's probably a good thing the doctor didn't know about this jumble of thoughts going on in my head. He might have been tempted to say, "Your heart is fine, but your head's a mess. I'm sending you straight to the psychiatric ward."

A FAMILIAR PLACE

It wouldn't have been the first time, of course. Fifteen years ago, as I was trying to put the pieces of my broken life back together again, I spent two weeks at a mental-health treatment center in St. Louis. The Christian clinic was part of a nationwide group of facilities offering treatment through a program developed by physicians in partnership with Christian psychologist Stephen Arterburn.

Although it was my own choice to be admitted there, my

time at the clinic did not begin pleasantly. When I arrived at the clinic, I decided not to go in. Then I did go in—and immediately decided to leave. Then I returned. It was totally exhausting and emotionally draining. Before that day was over, I found myself sitting on the floor in the corner of my room feeling completely lost, empty, and worthless.

I know *now* that my first day there followed a scenario that is completely typical and predictable. Two of my close friends, Christian comedienne Chonda Pierce and Women of Faith speaker and singer Sheila Walsh, describe their own floor time at the psychiatric hospital in similar ways. Like me, they sought help to regain their footing when the deepest, darkest depression imaginable shoved them over the edge into what felt like a bottomless abyss.

Like me, Chonda and Sheila are devout Christians who had put Jesus front and center in their lives for as long as they could remember. And yet, like me, they found themselves surrounded by an impenetrable darkness, unable to find the Light. I was flailing as I fell, futilely trying to swim through thin air. I was crying out for help, and when God answered I was like the man in Gene Anderson's joke, asking, "Is anybody *else* up there?"

Ironically, all of us were at the top of our game when the darkness descended. Sheila was cohosting a daily talk show on nationwide Christian television. Chonda was drawing huge crowds to a busy schedule of shows that combined Christian comedy and music. I'd been honored with a substantial number of Christian and secular music awards.

Yet there we huddled, on the floor of a psychiatric

hospital, totally overcome by misery and despair. That's the thing about depression. It makes no sense at all. I think that's why I felt so lost when I ended up there. Everything I knew to be true was still true, yet somehow it didn't help me to remember it.

Marilyn Meberg has said that depression clings to you like a wet shower curtain. That's a great mental image for me; it describes how I feel when I'm all tangled up in some clingy unpleasant feelings that won't go away. You can't just "shake off" those feelings on your own. You have to have help.

Profound feelings of failure and shame exist there on the floor of the psychiatric hospital, there on the wilderness side of the Jordan. One person described it as feeling like a zero with the rim rubbed out. What a gift it is when God sends an angel—whether it's a friend, a pastor, a counselor, or a physician—to lead us back across to the promised land, where, on our way to the abundant and rewarding life he wants us to have, we pass by a pile of rocks. An altar. There we remember again, *Oh, yeah. God was faithful here. And now he's faithful again.*

Frankly, we have to hope that we don't have to stand there at that altar again in the future, dripping with river water and smudged with the muck of yet another failure, and be reminded of God's faithfulness yet another time. But if you're like me, you know in your heart that you *will* make other visits to that pile of rocks. You also know that it'll be God's grace that gets you there—and then moves you past it, across that edge and into the divine.

WHAT MATTERS MOST

I read a comment somewhere that explains our Christian faith in the simplest terms: It's not what you've done that matters. It's what you do *next*. After that little pit stop in the emergency room, that pause beside the pile of rocks, I came away with an amazingly different mind-set that would guide me in how I responded *next*.

I'd told the doctor that the stress in my life stemmed from my illogical attitude that there just wasn't enough of me to go around. Those words triggered in me an amazing rush of thoughts and determination that went back to a speech I'd heard a few weeks earlier.

As part of his new job, which involves connecting to the surrounding community through outreach projects on behalf of his company, Don was invited to a charity dinner to benefit a wonderful Oklahoma organization called A Chance to Change. I got to go along as his new smaller-sized arm candy.

A Chance to Change is a nonprofit organization that operates an addiction treatment center focusing on helping the entire family. Its programs assist those affected by substance abuse, behavioral addictions, depression, anxiety, post-traumatic stress syndrome, marital and family issues, and a host of other problems. It's widely recognized as a tremendously effective resource, and that night at the dinner, the ACTC foundation was recognizing one of its own best resources, a man named Zane Fleming. The organization named Zane its man of the year for 2009.

In its own tribute to him, the *Edmond Sun* thanked Zane for "taking your personal experiences and turning them into a passion for helping others." That's the kind of great guy he is.

In his speech to us that night, Zane shared his own journey through sobriety. It was a journey he had resolutely continued for twenty-eight years, he said, even when his son, Nate, was killed in 2004 in the crash of a plane carrying members of the Oklahoma State University basketball team.

He talked about how, when you're an addict, you always think one more drink will be enough—one more pill or one more bet or one more of whatever it is that's controlling you. You think, *Just one more, and I won't want another.*

A dictionary definition of *enough* is "adequate for the want or need, sufficient." But the harsh reality is that *nothing* is ever enough, Zane said, until you understand that *God* is enough. Until we reach that point, nothing else will ever be sufficient.

When we *do* understand, however, our whole perspective suddenly changes.

As I left the hospital that night, pondering my feeling that there just wasn't enough of me to go around, I remembered Zane Fleming's words at the charity dinner. There wasn't enough alcohol in the world to satisfy his thirst, to heal the hurt of losing his son, to keep him going when he faced his own wilderness experiences. But God was there, and God was enough, he said.

I remembered how he had turned to his family at the

dinner that night and told them, "You are enough," and how he had turned to his wife, Ann, and said, "Honey, you are enough." Then he bowed his head and said, "Heavenly Father, you are enough."

He could have left it there, and his speech still would have been "enough" to leave a strong impact on me. Instead, he took it one step further and said, in a voice so humble and true, the words that brought it all home: "And God, I know that I am enough for you," he said.

IMMEASURABLE VALUE

As I left the hospital that night, so many seemingly contradictory thoughts were swirling through my head:

There just wasn't enough of me to go around . . . but I felt stronger, more confident and more capable than I'd ever felt before.

I tried and tried and tried every day to be everything my kids, my husband, my job, and my friends needed me to be; yet despite my best efforts, most nights I went to bed feeling like a failure because I hadn't done enough.

Then another pair of contradictory statements came to mind, two verses from the New Testament. First were the familiar words of John 3:16: "For God so loved the world that he gave his one and only Son, that whoever believes in him shall not perish but have eternal life" (NIV). Right on top of those words, another verse came tumbling into my memory, the amazing statement recorded in Romans 5:6:

"We can understand someone dying for a person worth dying for . . . But God put his love on the line for us by offering his Son in sacrificial death while we were of no use whatever to him."

So there's the greatest contradiction of all: we are so valuable to God that he sent his one and only Son to die for us—even though we are totally useless to him! Hmm. Do you suppose that might mean God doesn't base our value on what we can *do* for him? Do you suppose maybe Zane is right, and we're *enough* for God just as we are?

Could it be that he loves us so much, not for what we do, but for who—or rather, for *whose*—we are?

And since, as Christians, we're taught to love one another as he loves us, could it possibly be that, just as I'm enough for God simply because of his great and gracious love for me, I'm also enough for my husband and kids and family and friends in exactly the same way?

And could it be that God is enough for *them* as well?

What a freeing thought—that I don't have to "fix" everything for my family; I don't have to resolve all the problems and make everything perfect. Despite my Superwoman cape, I just can't do it. But if I believe that I am enough for God and he is enough for me, then the same is true for those dear ones in my life. They are enough for God, and he is enough for them.

Earlier in this book I talked about how the counseling before my Lap-Band surgery helped me understand that I had to recognize my own value before I could be successful in the challenge I was facing. Before I could permanently change my size and regain my health, I had to feel like I was *worth* the work it was going to take to reach that goal. As Don drove me home from the emergency room that night and that turbulent tornado of thoughts and ideas swirled through my mind, I finally and completely "got it."

Shortly after that day, something happened that felt like a little gift of grace to help me celebrate my newfound enlightenment. I was out on the road somewhere, traveling on the bus again. To pass the time, I'd brought along a bag of stuff that had gotten jumbled up together when we'd moved to Oklahoma.

One of the things in the jumble was a small, old, velvet bag with a drawstring top. Over the years I'd used it to carry a multitude of different things, and when we left Indiana, I'd spotted it in one of the drawers and tossed it in the bigger bag of stuff to be sorted through . . . someday. Now, as the miles rolled by outside the bus windows, I decided "someday" had come, and I started going through the larger bag, lifting out the various boxes and bags and deciding what to keep, what to throw away, what to send back home, and what I could use on the road.

When I got to the old velvet bag, it felt completely empty, and I started looking through the already-sorted things, thinking I might put some of them inside the velvet bag.

Then I cupped the bottom of the little bag in my palm and realized there was something in it after all. I stuck my hand through the loosened drawstring, and the minute my fingers touched the object inside, I let out a shriek that nearly caused our bus driver to run off the road.

It was the diamond ring Don had given me for our anniversary all those years earlier. The lost had been found. And lost. And then, after another two years, found again.

GRACE HAPPENS

Finding the ring again reminded me of the typical Christian's spiritual journey: three steps forward, two steps back . . . four steps forward, one step back . . . and so it goes. We keep trying, keep moving in the right direction, knowing that our journey isn't about a stopwatch but about a compass.

For many of us, those backward steps are the most precious because they're the ones that teach us about God's amazing grace. In my opinion, *forgiveness* is just about the best thing God ever dreamed up. It's right up there with love, faithfulness, and peace, if you ask me, and they're all intricately linked. God loves us so much he forgives us our sins when we sincerely repent of our mistakes. Knowing that forgiveness is one of his promises, we can live in a state of grace, which gives us peace.

We don't have to be afraid we'll make a mistake and be lost forever. We're not just the lost and found. We're the lost and found and lost and found *again*. Isn't that glorious?! Isn't that enough to make you want to dance down the church aisle and shout, "Thank you, Jesus!"? And isn't it enough to make you want to pass on that same grace to those around you who also make mistakes?

Uh, well, not so much.

Sometimes it's much easier to beg for our own forgiveness and celebrate God's grace than it is to grant that same forgiveness and grace to others, isn't it? Forgiving others isn't as easy as it looks!

I cherished the gracious way Don forgave me for losing the ring he'd scrimped and saved to buy me. But when it was my turn to extend that same grace, it didn't come as naturally as it did for him.

After we moved to Oklahoma, there were dozens of boxes of *stuff*. A lot of the boxes loaded with nonessential items ended up in the garage of our new house to be unpacked as time allowed. If you've ever moved, you know how it goes.

Gradually the stack of boxes diminished until one was left. It held my "show clothes," the glamorous outfits I wear onstage during special symphony concerts and the Christmas tour. Even more important, it held several pairs of, if I may say, absolutely fabulous shoes. During the year, I'd been working mostly with Women of Faith, a much more casual setting, so I hadn't needed the fancy stuff. That's why, by the beginning of winter, the show clothes and fabulous shoes were still in the box, still in the garage, still waiting to be unpacked.

Every time I parked the car in the garage I would see the box and think, *I've got to get those things out and get them ready to go before the concert season starts.* Some of them had been custom-made for me, and all of them were too expensive to just throw out. But they were way too big now and would need altering before I could wear them. Besides, I knew I wouldn't need them until winter when I did the Christmas and symphony concerts.

Meanwhile, back at the ranch (I don't know why, but Don likes to call our new home "the ranch," even though we're smack-dab in the middle of suburbia; now we all say it, even when, as in this case, it means simply *inside the house*), I was arranging things and filling up the closets. Our new house is much smaller than our Indiana house was, so I've had to do quite a bit of *downsizing*. I used to hate that word, but now that I'm eighty pounds lighter, I just love it!

As the seasons changed and I unpacked my fall and winter clothes, I realized a lot of them would no longer fit. Most of them weren't worth the cost of alterations, so those things I could no longer wear went into another box that I intended to give to the local Salvation Army thrift store.

After I'd filled it up, I set the box out in the garage, planning to take it to the Salvation Army later. Neither box was accurately labeled. The reused Salvation Army box said something like "master bathroom towels," I think. The show clothes box *was* labeled, but the box had been turned upside down, and the label was now on the bottom. *I* knew what was in the box, but the only thing visible identified the box's original contents, something like Charmin tissue.

Are you getting the drift of where this story is going?

Both boxes sat there for several weeks. Every time I drove into the garage, I'd have two thoughts as I saw them: *I need to take that box to the Salvation Army*, and *I need to go through my show clothes and get them altered.* A lot of times, we were all in the car together, and I would say something like, "Oh, I keep forgetting to take that box to the Salvation Army. I really need to do that."

Then one day I came home after being on the road a couple of days. I parked my car in the garage and noticed immediately that something looked different. Only one box was there. The Salvation Army box.

A big knot formed in my small stomach. I desperately hoped I would open the door to the kitchen and find the box of show clothes waiting there, maybe as a subtle hint from Don that I needed to get to work on that project of sorting and altering. But the show clothes box wasn't in the kitchen, wasn't in the bedroom, wasn't anywhere.

Don was at work, and I fumbled with my cell phone. I couldn't get to his speed-dial number fast enough. "Don, did you take my box of show clothes to the Salvation Army?" I yelled as soon as he said hello.

"No, I took the box of Salvation Army stuff to the Salvation Army," he said slowly, starting to sound wary. "At least I thought I did."

"Did you not see that one box was clearly labeled 'master bathroom towels' and the other one said Charmin tissue?"

"What?" Now the poor man was really confused, and my babbling about bathroom tissue wasn't helping any. "Sandi, I didn't see anything that said show clothes."

We then shared a moment of silence, absorbing the impact of what had happened.

"Don! How could you do that? You should have asked me first. What were you thinking?"

"I'm sorry, honey. I thought I was doing you a favor," he said. "I'm really sorry."

"When did you take it? Maybe I can still get them back," I said.

"I took them the day you left. That was, what? Three, four days ago? Honey, I'm sorry. I'm *really* sorry. I'm sure they're out in the store by now. Maybe I could go down there and try to buy them back for you."

"Right! Like *that's* going to happen," I growled. "That's just *great*, Don. Thank you *so* much for *helping* me."

I pushed the END button, plopped into a chair, and held my head in my hands. I was so mad at Don, I couldn't see straight. I hated to think how much it would cost to replace those beaded, glitzy outfits, not to mention the fabulous shoes that *did* still fit.

Then some other imaginings came into my mind. I pictured the Salvation Army worker opening that box and pulling out the first dress. In my mind, I saw her thinking, *Wow, this is really pretty.* (Okay, she might also think, *Wow, this is really BIG.*)

Then I pictured her calling over her supervisor to see the pretty clothes in the box. I thought about how she would take them to the formalwear rack of the thrift store. Then I imagined some lucky plus-size woman flipping through the rack.

Maybe she'd felt a little blue that day, a little frustrated because she had a special event to go to and she needed a dress but couldn't afford anything fancy. Maybe she had come into the thrift store, not really expecting to find anything suitable in her size, but with just a tiny spark of hope.

Then I pictured her coming upon my show clothes, hanging there on the rack. *Oh, look at this*, she might think, seeing the beads and sequins, the luxurious fabric.

The imagined scene lifted my mood.

Then I thought of how Don must feel. Lower than dirt, I suspected.

And wouldn't you know? Just as I was having those thoughts, my eye happened to fall on . . .

The ring.

Now it was my turn to feel lower than dirt.

FINDING THINGS TO LIKE

Jesus told us, "From everyone who has been given much, much will be demanded; and from the one who has been entrusted with much, much more will be asked" (Luke 12:48 NIV). I've been given *so* much. So much forgiveness, so many blessings. Now, here I was, fuming over a box of stupid clothes.

I pushed the speed-dial button again. "I'm so sorry for snapping at you," I told Don. "Can you please forgive me? Thank you for taking that stuff to the Salvation Army. I've been thinking about it, and the truth is, I'm *glad* you took the wrong box. I'm nearly five sizes smaller now; some of those clothes were 24s, and I'm wearing

14s now. I couldn't have had them altered anyway. It's just too big a difference. I say, Good riddance to those old show clothes!"

To be honest, I didn't have quite as gracious an attitude about the fabulous shoes. But, oh well. What's done is done.

Don laughed. "I suppose this means you'll be going shopping now," he said.

"Absolutely!" I said.

"Do I need to start the application for a second mortgage?"

I assured him I wouldn't need quite that much–but I *would* be going shopping. That brought to my mind a whole new set of images.

Shopping used to be a dreaded activity for me. Plussize women don't have a whole lot of choices out there in the marketplace; only a handful of specialty stores offer attractive clothing in larger sizes. Meanwhile, shopping for plus sizes in regular department stores forces larger women to encounter what is surely the most thoughtless marketing idea there ever could be: the plus sizes are usually displayed right next to petites.

Really, folks. Does that make sense? Does someone think we *like* walking by those tiny little mannequins and cute little shoppers as we make our way to double-digit sizes with all those Xs and Ls added onto them? Don't get me started! Okay, well, it's too late; I'm already started. I'm sorry, but I just think that whole idea of plus-sizes-next-to-petites is so wrong. That's definitely going on my list of things to ask God about when I get to heaven–that, and menstrual cramps. I mean, what is the point?

Remember how I told you that now I no longer stuff down my feelings with food, they sometimes come exploding out of my mouth–or, in this case, out of my fingertips–to become words that can hurt feelings and get me in trouble? Well, assuming that my editor doesn't take them out and you're reading them here, this is a perfect example of how those little incidents happen. It also explains why for many years I had avoided the department stores and shopped for clothes in places like Lane Bryant and Dress Barn Woman and Avenue.

As my weight dropped, the clothes from plus-size specialty shops stopped working for me. My last purchase from Lane Bryant was several months ago, when I bought a pair of jeans in the smallest size they offer. Now they're too big for me.

This drop in sizes has opened a whole new universe for me because, guess what: now I can go shopping with my girls! The six of us can go shopping together and look at things on the same racks. Well, okay, we're looking at opposite ends of the same rack, but still, we're hanging out together, and I'm in the department stores with them, shopping in misses sizes, and I love that.

Well, I love it most of the time, at least. The truth is, sometimes it's a little overwhelming. I mean, I used to go into my favorite Lane Bryant store and find what I needed right there in that one place. Now nearly every store in the mall has clothes I can wear. And believe me, if my girls had their way we *would* go into all of them. As I hang out with them, I'm quickly realizing how easy it could be to swap a food addiction for a shopping addiction if I don't stay alert and strong.

I hate that need for vigilance, honestly. But we are a work in progress, pressing on toward the goal of being made complete when we see Jesus. In the meantime we are responsible for showing up each day and making the right next choice. Sometimes that means closing the refrigerator door. Sometimes it means stepping away from the shoe department at Dillard's.

Here's something funny. When my girls and I go to the department store, I still find myself looking for the women's section. They're trying to retrain me, though. They see my head swiveling around, looking for the sign, and say, "Mom, stop looking for the plus sizes. The misses section is right here at the top of the escalator."

This past Christmas, when the whole family was gathered and we were opening presents, I found a beautiful gift-wrapped box, sort of a large shirt box, addressed to me from my beautiful girls. As soon as I picked it up, I felt just a tiny twinge of nervousness. I could tell it was something soft, and I suspected that it was clothes. *But what if it's too small?* I thought. *It'll mean they think I'm not losing weight fast enough.*

Obviously, that old habit of second-guessing and "hearing" totally wrong, unspoken messages hadn't completely been put to rest yet.

I tore off the paper and looked at the box. *Banana*

Republic. Oh, dear. Their stuff is so small. I don't think they even carry 14s, do they?

I lifted the lid and found a couple of absolutely beautiful tops–knit pullover shirts in colors I love. Then I saw the size tags. *I'll just slip back to the store tomorrow and exchange them,* I thought.

I smiled and gushed and thanked my girls for such a beautiful gift. "I *love* them!" I said.

But Anna has a gift for hearing unspoken messages too. Fortunately, she tends to sense messages that are closer to being true. She could see that I thought the shirts were too small.

"Mom, try them on," she said. "Let us see how they look on you."

"Oh, I'll try them on later," I told her. "I really do *love* them–love those colors."

"Try them on!" the other girls said. It became a chorus of commands.

Finally, feeling I had no choice and preparing myself for the disappointed looks I would soon see on their faces, I took the shirts into the bedroom. I took off the blouse I was wearing and pulled the first shirt over my head, expecting to have to twist and squirm my way into it.

It fit *perfectly*!

I came prancing out of the bedroom like a showgirl struttin' my stuff, as happy as a dog who's just dug up something wonderful and then comes bouncing and twisting into the house to show it off to family and friends. I jumped up and down, modeling my new outfit, squealing and hugging my girls. "Can you believe this?" I exclaimed.

"Mom, you just don't realize how much smaller you are now," Erin said. "You look *really* good."

Well, of course her opinion was a little biased, but slowly, I was starting to believe it. I'm finally starting to see myself with a new appreciation for the work God and I, with a surgeon's help, are doing in my body.

My friend Anita Renfroe had played a hand in my attitude change too, way back there in the beginning, before my surgery. Like my pal Chonda, Anita is also a wise and witty Christian comedienne. I laughed my way through her book *If You Can't Lose It, Decorate It*, and for a long time I had claimed one of her best lines as my own. "The average woman in America is a size 14," Anita says. "And who wants to be below average?"

Anita advises women with a poor body-image attitude to start by identifying *one thing* they like about themselves. Everybody has *something*, she says. Identify it and thank God for it. Show it off a little bit.

Anita and I were both doing Women of Faith conferences at the time, and one day after she'd said that to an audience somewhere, I sent her a text message. "By the way," I said, "I like my ankles."

It was true. I *do* like my ankles. I've always liked the way they look when I put on high heels. When everything else about me was big, my ankles seemed, well, small and demure.

It wasn't much, I know, but it was a start.

The next weekend we were speaking again at Women

of Faith. Anita sat down next to me at breakfast that morning and slid a little package across the table. "I brought you
something," she said with mischief twinkling in her eye.

It was an ankle bracelet.

You know what? Something magical happened when I
snapped that little piece of "decoration" around my ankle.
I'm not sure how to describe exactly what it was, but somehow I felt a little prettier, a little more confident. That
little piece of decoration helped me remember that parts
of me were A-OK.

In order to show off the ankle bracelet, I found myself
wearing cute dresses and skirts and more stylish cropped
pants. I was dressing a little better, and that made me feel
better. I started looking for other things I liked about myself.

I thought, well, I've always liked my hands, especially
when I'm wearing that gorgeous ring my man bought me!
I like my smile. And my hair . . .

One little thought at a time, my thinking evolved into
the powerful belief that I'm worth whatever it takes to feel
this good about *all* of myself. How does that old saying
go? "I know I'm worth it 'cause God don't make no junk!"
That new attitude played a big part in my decision to go
ahead with the surgery and work hard to get healthy.

Now I was well on my way–and I had the credentials to
prove it. A few months after we moved to Oklahoma, I got
a new driver's license. And this one has my correct weight
on it, thank you very much!

Then something else happened. It was a little thing,
something most people wouldn't even notice, but it was

enough to put a smile on my face that lasted all day. I was getting on a plane for yet another trip and was making my way down the aisle to my window seat. A man was sitting in the aisle seat beside mine, and I paused, smiled, and said the usual, "Sorry to bother you. I'm by the window."

Here's the cool thing that happened: *the man moved his knees to the side to let me slip by him.*

It took me a second to realize what he had done. He simply moved his knees to the side and let me slip by. Sorry. I know I'm being redundant here, but it was such a wonderful moment for me, I just keep thinking about it.

I can't remember the last time I claimed my window seat on an airplane when the other seat (sometimes two seats) were already occupied and my fellow passengers didn't stand up and step into the aisle to let me by. Sometimes they did so with an annoyed look on their faces, which I second-guessed as meaning they were annoyed that they had to sit by an oversized passenger. But on that trip, for the first time in memory, my seatmate glanced up, smiled at me, and *moved his knees to the side to let me slip by.*

Okay, I'll try not to say it again. But seriously, it was all I could do to keep from leaning down and kissing him when I happily settled into my seat.

CARNEGIE HALL

As 2009's Women of Faith tour wound to a close, my Christmas concert tour began. The schedule had my band

and me performing, sometimes alone and sometimes with local orchestra and choral groups, in nearly thirty cities around the country. Two of those dates, near the end of the tour, were at Carnegie Hall in New York City, where we would appear with the New York City Pops Orchestra and the Young People's Chorus of New York.

Every time I looked at the tour schedule and saw those words, I felt like I was living in a fairy tale. It wasn't my first-ever appearance at Carnegie Hall. I'd performed there with the Gaither Homecoming program a few years earlier, and I'd participated in a fund-raising gala for the New York City Pops. But this was the first time my name and picture appeared along with the NYC Pops on the billboard outside the famed facility. As a performer, it's simply the dream of all dreams to have that happen.

And it wasn't just the billboard out front. Oh, no! I had some pretty amazing advance publicity going for me as well. One of my friends was in New York, dining out with friends in one of the many fabulous restaurants. When he was in the men's room, he noticed that someone had written on the wall, in quite lovely graffiti, "Sandi Patty @ Carnegie Hall Dec. 18-19."

Now *that* is some powerful PR, let me tell you!

My family was really happy for me, as you can imagine, especially my parents. Dad had performed in New York City back in the late 1950s when he was traveling with Fred Waring and the Pennsylvanians. The Fred Waring concert is my earliest memory of seeing Dad sing with that group, which was wildly popular at the time. I was just a toddler, but I understood that it was a really big deal.

Don would be singing a song with me during the two Carnegie concerts, so he was there; Anna and Collin, Mollie, Jenn, and Sam were in the audience. It was such an exciting time.

We arrived in the city on Thursday and prepared for Friday afternoon's open rehearsal, which means Carnegie opened our dress rehearsal to a selected group of patrons. I've always enjoyed dress rehearsals with an orchestra as much as, if not more than, the actual performance. It's just a bit more casual, but that doesn't mean everyone's not perfectly prepared and ready to go.

Being prepared was especially important for my band and me as we began our work at Carnegie Hall. We wanted to show those professional musicians that we are professional Christian musicians who understand the orchestra world; we respect that whole system. We came to that rehearsal very well prepared; we knew our stuff, and we were ready to go.

When you perform with an orchestra, you're expected to dress a little differently and have a more formal appearance. We knew to do that. And we knew there are customary things to do when working with an orchestra. For example, it's important to thank the conductor, in this case the talented John Morris Russell. It's also really important to thank and shake hands with the concertmaster, who is usually the first-chair violinist. It's something that's usually done during rehearsal or on stage during the performance.

Typically, the thank you comes after the orchestra plays a song particularly well. (With the New York City Pops, it's impossible to say one sounds better than another; everything they play is absolutely fabulous.) In between songs, as the musicians are adjusting their music, I just slip over and shake the concertmaster's hand and express my gratitude, briefly but sincerely, for a job well done. By thanking the concertmaster, I'm thanking the whole orchestra. It's such a little thing to do, but it means a lot to everyone involved. I've learned, over the years, that if the concertmaster is with me and is invested in helping me look good, then the rest of the orchestra is too.

When we're doing a closed rehearsal and there's no audience, I like to face the orchestra. It lets me make eye contact with my fellow performers so I know who I'm going to have to win over and who's going to have an attitude. I do love that intimate time of getting acquainted with the symphony and coming together to put on the best possible concert we can.

During the New York rehearsal I was also able to chat for a few moments with the high school students in the Young People's Chorus of New York, letting them know how much I appreciated the work they had done to get to that level. After all, it's quite a commitment for high school kids to show up again and again to learn and practice the kind of music involved in a symphony performance. I was glad to get a chance to brag on them a little and encourage them.

Rehearsal went well, and a few hours later, the house

lights went down, the stage lights came up, and the concert itself began. I waited backstage for my cue, listening in awe to the orchestra's introductory piece and thinking, *Man! They sure sound better than those records I used to sing with as a young girl performing along to my little record player!*

But the truth was, the heart of that little girl dancing and singing alone in her little bedroom all those years ago is the same heart that walked out on that stage at Carnegie Hall. It's a heart full to bursting with the joy of music and an appreciation for its language, its ability to speak for me when I couldn't find the words, the gift it's been to me all my life. On my journey back to good health, I'm regaining something else that's wonderful. I've fallen in love with music all over again. Never were those feelings stronger than when I stepped onto the stage at Carnegie Hall.

The New York Pops is a massive orchestra. Relatively speaking, the Carnegie Hall stage is small. A singer performing with the Pops stands right at the front of that stage.

Right at the edge.

Standing there on December 18 was one of the most thrilling things I've ever done as a musician. It represented so much more than a sold-out concert. Not so much "look at me I've finally made it," but an acknowledgment of my long season of experience.

You've probably heard that old story about the wandering tourist who asked directions of a famous pianist he happened to meet on a New York City sidewalk. Not recognizing the great musician, the tourist inquired, "Sir, do you know how to get to Carnegie Hall?"

"Practice, practice, practice!" the great pianist replied.

For more than thirty years, I had practiced, practiced, practiced my craft. I've done this singing thing in tiny churches and grand settings. But to perform in Carnegie Hall is every musician's dream, right up there at the top of the wish list. The edge of Carnegie's stage is not where you refine your work. It's the place where you'd better be prepared.

We have a little saying in our family: "Go big or go home." (Actually, now that I'm doing some personal downsizing, I've suggested we change it to "Go *bold* or go home.") For me, standing on that edge at Carnegie Hall incorporated both the recognition of my past experience and the "point at which something is likely to begin." It felt like the celebration of a new beginning: A new, healthier body. A new chapter of my work as a performer. And, an all-encompassing thankfulness to the One who has made it all possible, a closer relationship to my Savior.

BEYOND THE SPOTLIGHT

Maybe you think that after an open rehearsal and an evening concert in a single day at Carnegie Hall, we would stagger back to our hotel in triumphant exhaustion and head off to Dreamland. But no! There was one more amazing event to be experienced—and it happened around midnight.

I don't have to tell you that New York City is the heart of live theater in America. Just as Carnegie Hall is the epitome of a musician's career, Broadway is the pinnacle for actors, dancers, singers, musicians, and everyone else involved in live theater. That group of super-talented people is amazingly diverse, with a tremendously wide range of backgrounds, gifts, and lifestyles. Some of them come together each week for a fun and creative tradition called The After Party. It always has a theme, often focusing on someone who is performing in the city.

The "party"–it's actually more like a show–begins after all the Broadway people have finished work in the many plays and events around town on Friday nights. That's why it starts so late. The program is a cross between a tribute and a roast, featuring delightful music and hilarious comedy. Anyone can come; the program is kind of an open-microphone thing where anyone can sing or talk a couple of minutes. The only rule is you have to stick to the theme designated for that night.

At least I think that's an accurate description of The After Party. I've only been to one, the zany and heartwarming event organized in my honor by The After Party's host, singer Brandon Cutrell, and maestro Ray Fellman after my performance at Carnegie Hall.

To tell the truth, I wasn't sure I would or should go. You can imagine how tired I was, and also, I knew that those New York City theater people can get pretty wild and bawdy when they really let their hair down, which is what The After Party is designed to let them do. But the more I heard about it, the more appealing it became–especially when I heard that Brandon, a longtime fan of mine, had flown in his mother from Indiana for the occasion. *Well,* I thought, *if he's bringing his mother, surely it won't be too crazy.* Since he was doing so much work to organize an event spotlighting my New York City appearances, I thought the least I could do was show up, say a brief thank you, and then head on back to the hotel.

So the band, Don, the kids, and I went and we stayed until the end. We had such a good time and enjoyed it so much, we simply couldn't tear ourselves away, even as the hour grew later and later.

The After Party is set in the Laurie Beechman Theatre in the basement of the West Bank Café, and that night it was standing room only, with people even watching from the stairs. I was stunned by the late-night turnout. The performers took their turns at the microphone, and I was totally blown away by what we heard.

One by one, the singers and actors told how they were connected to me through their memories and experiences, and then they sang songs I had performed or recorded sometime in my career. Some of them talked about being in the children's fan club, the Friendship Company, that operated nationwide during my early career. Or they remembered how, at a concert somewhere, I'd invited all the children to join me for a song or two, and they'd jumped out of their seats and run up to the stage. Or maybe they'd been asked to sing, alone or with their families, one of my songs for their church or some other group. One of them said, "Sandi, every Sunday morning I would wake up and sing your songs with my family."

Oh, what a thrill to sit in that New York City basement and hear some of Broadway's most talented voices sing the songs that had meant so much to me for so long: "Bethlehem Morning," "Amazing Grace," "Via Dolorosa," "How Great Thou Art," and a dozen more. One performer lip-synched "Twinkle Twinkle Little Star" from my recording decades earlier on one of the children's albums.

I even got to sing along with a couple of them. Singing "For Good" with Kristy Cates, who has starred in the musical *Wicked* on Broadway as well as in Toronto and Chicago, was absolutely a dream come true. For just a moment, there in my mind, I was on Broadway too!

And what laughter! At one point Brandon unloaded a grocery bag full of my record albums (yes, *albums*. You know—big CDs) to present a tongue-in-cheek review of my big-haired, rhinestone-sprinkled, puffy-sleeved church-lady fashion choices over the years. He examined one album-cover photo after another, eyebrows raised, face twisted, cracking witty, outrageous comments about each spectacular hairstyle and frock.

Clearly my fashion sense was not what had inspired these loyal fans.

There were poignant moments, too. One of the performers spoke from the heart when he said that most of us in that room, at one time or another, had been misjudged or misunderstood. "Sandi, tonight we just want you to know, when so many others said you were done, we knew your best days were still ahead of you. And here you are, singing at Carnegie Hall, looking better than you've ever looked, sounding better than you've ever sounded, ministering more than you could ever possibly imagine."

I have to tell you, I've received a lot of awards in my life, but that night, hearing those stories made an even bigger impact on my heart. Music has been the medium that has helped me express what I held inside, and to hear that my music had touched other people's lives and hearts in certain times in their lives . . . it was one of the most meaningful, spiritually rich moments I can remember in my career.

Don put it best as we were (finally!) heading back to the hotel in the wee hours of the morning. He called it "a strangely holy moment."

TAKING NEW YORK BY STORM

The second night's concert at Carnegie was also sold out, but there was a problem. Saturday morning, weather forecasters were warning that a powerful blizzard was barreling down on New York. Every news report throughout the day warned that it was coming, coming, coming.

We held a team meeting. For the band and me, there was no question about it. Our philosophy was, the show goes on—unless Carnegie Hall says the show *doesn't* go on. There were just a few of us, and we could walk from the hotel to the concert hall. But the dozens of others involved in the show, including the students in the Young People's Chorus and the members of the orchestra, would be coming from all over the metropolitan area.

We eagerly went ahead with the concert, and to my amazement, only about a quarter of the seats were empty. God bless those hardy folks who ventured out in bad weather to be there that night, both to hear the music we were making and also to help make it!

When we left the hotel to head to Carnegie, the news stations were reporting that Long Island was already pretty much snowed under. As we stepped out onto the sidewalk in Manhattan, flakes were beginning to flutter through the air. And by the time the show ended and we headed back to the hotel, a full-fledged blizzard had engulfed us. We could barely see fifty feet in front of us as we leaned into the howling wind and near-white-out conditions and made our way back the block and a half to the welcoming warmth of our temporary home.

OVER THE TOP

It was hard to imagine that the New York experience could ever be topped. But then, after Christmas, our whole family gathered in Florida for a wild and wonderful Disney adventure, and I'm not just talking about riding roller coasters. What happened in Orlando became another edge, another point where something was likely to begin–and *did* begin. It was another amazing step in my journey toward health and fitness.

When you go through major life changes, little things can take on new significance. For me, one of those little things happened every time I stepped onto the stage at Women of Faith conferences. In these arenas, the regular speakers sit on a floor-level platform nicknamed "The Porch," which is connected to the stage by a set of five or six steps. As each speaker is introduced, she climbs those steps, strides onto the stage, and begins her presentation.

It's a very simple thing, climbing those steps, striding onto the stage, and beginning your performance–unless you have health challenges. Eighty pounds ago, climbing those steps and going right into my first fast-tempo song was like climbing Mount Everest and immediately beginning a break-dance routine. I wanted to bounce up the steps like little live-wire Patsy Clairmont does. I wanted to move energetically around the stage, clapping my hands and singing and bringing the audience with me into the upbeat spirit of the music.

But eighty pounds ago, that was *not* easy to do! It might have *looked* like I was trotting up the steps and immediately leading the audience into the energetic song, but what was actually happening was that I was pulling and pushing myself quickly up the steps using the handrail. When I got to the stage, I basically stood in one place, maybe turning around to all sides of the audience, clapping my hands, bobbing to the music, smiling–and *trying desperately to catch my breath!* Hurrying up that little set of steps and immediately going into a fast-tempo song was *really* hard for me physically, almost more than I could manage.

As my weight dropped, however, the challenge became easier. In fact, I remember one particular conference late in the year when I did the usual pull-and-push routine with the handrail, propelling myself up the steps, and I almost launched myself right off the far edge of the stage! I propelled myself to the top and just kept going!

What a strange and thrilling sensation that was. I finally *could* move around the stage and call out to the audience as we began the first song. It was an amazing and exhilarating moment.

Many more of those moments occurred as the year came to a close, including some events I could have never even imagined possible not too long ago. For one thing, I participated in my first athletic competition since high school.

Well, for most of the participants, it wasn't a real competition, but if you'll indulge me, that's how I want to think of the 2010 Disney Marathon.

Okay, just to keep things honest, I didn't run the marathon. Or even the mini-marathon. But I *did* complete the 5K run–3.1 miles–which might as well have been a marathon, in my opinion. They called it a "fun run," which seemed like a total oxymoron to me when we signed up, as a family, a full year before the event. But guess what: I had fun!

It all happened thanks to Anna's handsome, smart, athletic husband, Collin.

Our family loves Disney World. Different members in our family have worked there in the musical shows or special events, and we just really feel at home there. It's such an awesome thing to see this happen so many years after I thought my life had just about ended because I didn't get selected for Kids of the Kingdom at Disneyland back in California.

A year ago, we planned a week of family time at Disney World, and that week would occur during the annual Disney Marathon and its related events. Anna and Collin suggested we sign up for some of those events. The two of them planned to do the mini-marathon. With great trepidation, I signed up for the 5K, along with Erin, Sam, Jonathan, and Jonathan's girlfriend, Mindy.

Think about it: when I signed up for that event, I was still about forty pounds heavier than I am now. I was still at the point where climbing the steps to the Women of Faith stage was a major "athletic event" for me. At that point I had probably only *walked* three miles a few times in my whole adult life, let alone *run* that far. Never, in my wildest dreams, had I considered that I might be able to do such a thing.

But my family saw how hard I was working to get healthy, and they helped me believe that what had been impossible in the past was indeed possible now—or would be in a year. "You can do it, Mom," Sam told me. "We'll help you."

I wasn't sure how other people could "help" me complete a 5K run, but I was willing to try. Still, as the months rolled by and the event grew nearer, I wasn't exactly a cauldron of confidence.

I still felt that trepidation the morning of the run. We had to be at the site at 5:30 a.m., even though the 5K didn't start until 7:00. More time to be nervous. Finally, the starter gun sounded, and I started out like gangbusters, thanks in part to encouraging high-fives from Mickey and Minnie Mouse and a bunch of other Disney characters. Don, Jenn,

Aly, and Mollie were on the sidelines too, cheering louder than anyone else. Disney employees volunteer for the marathon events, and they joined hundreds of family members and friends lining the course, cheering and urging on the participants, handing out cups of water and continually calling out, "Way to go!" and "Yaaaaaay!" and "Go, go, go!"

Jogging through all those cheering, encouraging people, I thought of Hebrews 12:1, the verse that says, "Since we are surrounded by such a great cloud of witnesses, let us throw off everything that hinders and the sin that so easily entangles, and let us run with perseverance the race marked out for us" (NIV). The *Message* Bible describes the encouragers as "pioneers who blazed the way, all these veterans cheering us on."

Still, despite all those friendly words of encouragement, I began to fade at about 2.5 miles. I wanted to finish strong, but I was *really* getting tired. With each step, my pace was slowing. I was starting to wind down—just when the finish line was so close. A lot of signals were going off in my body that said, *You have to stop!* But I just wouldn't let myself give up. I kept telling myself, *Thirty more seconds, twenty more steps, keep going, keep moving.*

I never stopped, but I slowed from a jog to a staggering walk. If I had been totally alone, I probably would have stopped, but just at the moment when I believed I wasn't going to make it, and just at the point when I thought I could not take one more step, Jonathan and Mindy came alongside and grabbed both my hands. "Come on, Mom! You can do this," Jonathan said.

His words sounded like what Eliphaz said to encourage Job when he was about to give up: "Your words have put stumbling people on their feet, put fresh hope in people about to collapse" (Job 4:4). They were just enough to keep me going.

The two of them probably would have dragged me the rest of the way if they'd had to. Fortunately, that wasn't necessary. It was enough that they merely continued to hold my hands, and together we ran "with perseverance the race marked out for us." They let go just in time for me to cross the finish line by myself, completely exhausted but totally thrilled.

At that glorious moment I felt like Rocky Balboa at the top of the art museum steps, although I didn't have the strength to dance around like Rocky did. In fact, I could barely lift one hand for a final high five. But in my heart, I was right up there with Rocky, struttin' my stuff, both arms raised in victory, yelling my heart out in triumph.

I'd heard people say that running a marathon affects your mind-set as much as your physical condition. In other words, like so many other challenges, maybe running a marathon is an "inside job." I'm still a long way from being a marathoner, but I do understand now what it means to have a marathon mind-set.

I understand that, for most contestants, a marathon isn't about competing with others; it's about racing against yourself, doing *your* best, not someone else's. Isn't that true in life as well? Running the 5K, I came to the edge of my endurance, and my body wanted to quit. But my heart and my head joined forces to keep me going. And just when *those* factors started to fade, Jonathan and Mindy came alongside me. Their encouragement and presence beside me were just enough to help me complete those last few steps.

What a celebration we had that week at Disney, commemorating our 5K finishes as well as Anna's and Collin's completion of the mini-marathon. But that wasn't all. We also celebrated Erin's and Mollie's birthdays, and then– what a momentous occasion–we celebrated Jonathan and Mindy's engagement. He surprised her by proposing during a family trip to Epcot.

Knowing that Mindy loves China and its culture, he set up a dinner that night for just the two of them at Epcot's Chinese pavilion. As they strolled through the beautiful Chinese gardens afterward, he dropped to one knee and proposed to Mindy. (I had made my own proposal, suggesting that the rest of us hide in the shrubbery to watch the big moment, but that proposal got nixed.)

Mindy said yes! Then, because Jonathan is the one who especially loves how music can give special meaning to any story, and also because Mindy is a music lover too, he had arranged things so that we all joined up again beside Epcot's lake to watch the nightly fireworks illumination, all perfectly coordinated with a beautiful, sweeping musical score.

So many happy thoughts filled my head as I stood there surrounded by my dearest loved ones. For most of his life, following that childhood brain injury, Jonathan may have wondered if he would be capable enough as an adult to live a full and rewarding life. But now here he was, about to finish college, aware of his gifts and his areas of struggle but also confident in his abilities. He's a bright young man with an even brighter future.

For most of *my* life, I'd believed I wasn't good enough, strong enough, fit enough to live the wide-open, falling-over-happy, healthy, guilt-free life God wanted for me. I certainly never felt capable of completing a challenge of physical endurance. I always *said* I wanted to do something like running a 5K, but my choices didn't reflect what I said my priorities were. Now that I'm running my own private race back to good health, my priorities and my choices are starting to match up. I'm learning to accept that the blessings God has given me are *enough* to achieve the goals he and I set for me.

I'm learning to believe that *God* is enough, and with him all things are possible.

And, by the way, I'm now training for a mini-marathon.

Believing Is Enough

Thousands of years ago, the prophet said, "The person in right standing before God through loyal and steady *believing* is fully alive, *really* alive" (Habbakuk 2:4, italics mine).

"Don't be afraid," Jesus said. "Just believe" (Mark 5:36 NIV). "Everything is possible for him who believes" (Mark 9:23 NIV). "Whoever believes in me has real life, eternal life" (John 6:47).

That's what we want, isn't it? *Real* life. That "real and eternal life, more and better life than [we] ever dreamed of"–the life Jesus described in John 10:10. Life abounding with good health and overflowing with love and happiness.

It's so easy to *say* that's what we want . . . yet sometimes it feels so very difficult to *do*. We seem to travel along a boundary, an edge, that separates us from God's divine, all-encompassing, and empowering love that will give us the abundantly wonderful life we desire. We want to throw our heart over that edge and then follow it right on over into God's everlasting arms. Yet there's something that holds us back.

It's sort of like saying it's easy to lose weight. All we have to do is . . . eat less. A little exercise helps too. So why is it so hard for us? Because it requires us to summon up the willpower to do what we know is right and refrain from doing what we know we shouldn't do. We have to make our actions match our priorities. Most importantly, we have to *commit*, knowing that "simple" act of commitment may require us to take on the difficult and painful challenges of changing our lives, our habits, our behavior, our minds.

And oh, change is so hard sometimes. Scary. Maybe we finally do commit, but with great trepidation. Then we start out like gangbusters. We relish the encouragement of others there at the beginning. We follow the path with enthusiasm and determination.

For a while.

Then exhaustion sets in. Weariness consumes us. We are on the verge of collapse, counting down the steps to failure. It's impossible to go farther. We're done.

And just then another Runner comes alongside us. "You can do it," he tells us, matching our stumbling steps with his confident ones. "By yourself it's impossible, but with me by your side *nothing* is impossible."

He doesn't drag us. We understand he's giving us a choice, not a command. He tells us we can finish the race and dance triumphantly at the finish line . . . if we choose to believe.

Just believe.

Jesus doesn't say it'll be easy, just that it'll be *enough*. We still have to run those last, grueling steps. But he promises never to leave us or forsake us; he'll be there with us to the end. And that's really all we need.

The Bible is alive with stories of men and women who chose to believe despite much harsher circumstances than those we face today. The writer to the Hebrews talks about believers who by faith "braved abuse and whips, and, yes, chains and dungeons. . . . were stoned, sawed in two, murdered in cold blood; stories of vagrants wandering the earth in animal skins, homeless, friendless, powerless–the world didn't deserve them!–making their way as best they could on the cruel edges of the world" (Hebrews 11:36–38).

Matthew 8 tells the story of a Roman centurion who believed. (A Roman! Just think what his shocked family, friends, and coworkers must have thought about what he was doing.) He rushed up to Jesus in Capernaum and begged him to heal his servant, who was sick at home, suffering terribly. Jesus told the Roman officer he would come to his home.

"'Oh, no,' said the captain. 'I don't want to put you to all that trouble. Just give the order and my servant will be fine'" (v. 8).

I believe, Jesus.

And with that, the servant was healed.

My favorite story is told in Luke 8:43–48. Maybe I identify with it because the main character is a woman who had struggled for years with a debilitating health problem. She'd tried every remedy she'd heard of, gone to every doctor she could find, spent all her money trying to find a way back to healthiness, but nothing had worked.

Then she heard about a man who was performing miracles and changing lives. Some people even said he was the Messiah.

Maybe she'd managed to attend some of the gatherings where he spoke. Maybe she simply pondered stories of others who shared what they'd heard and seen. We don't know anything about her life until that day when she fought her way through the crowd in Galilee.

Maybe the crowd was too big, too boisterous, for her to meet Jesus face-to-face. Maybe she was too sick, too weak, to get any farther. Maybe she'd been knocked down, trampled by the throng. Maybe she was simply shy, afraid to call attention to herself and her embarrassing problem.

We don't know how she ended up behind Jesus that

day. All we know is that *she believed*. And with that belief burning in her heart, she reached through the crowd and touched the edge of his robe.

And that was enough.

It's enough for each of us too.

Questions for Discussion and Individual Reflection

Overview

1. To set the tone for her book, Sandi chose Job 26:14 as the epigraph. The verse is attributed to the Old Testament character Job, who suffered devastating losses and overwhelming challenges. Read verses 5–13, the verses leading up to Job's declaration, which cite examples of God's all-powerful might and abilities, and then consider what God is able to do today—in the world and in your life.

Chapter 1. The Edge Between Despair and the Divine

1. In Psalm 38:19, the psalmist says he is "on the edge of losing it" and is "ready to tell my story of failure." What failure(s) have you experienced, and what brought you to the point of being ready to tell your story? What brought the psalmist—and perhaps you—to the point of being ready to share that experience?

2. Sandi's book begins with her description of a time when she felt her life was on the brink of disaster. Think of a time when you were on the edge of

physical calamity or emotional despair. (Or maybe you're there now!) Read John 8:26 and describe a situation where the Holy Spirit interceded for you when you couldn't summon the words.

3. Oswald Chambers wrote that, in good times and bad, God brings us "to places, among people, and into certain conditions to accomplish a definite purpose through the intercession of the Spirit in you." Think of a time or place when God put you "among people" who came alongside you and led you closer to the edge of the divine, helping you have a clearer understanding of God's will for your life.

4. When have you experienced what Oswald Chambers described as "the unexpected sacredness of circumstances"? How can you become more attuned to God's presence in your life, more aware of the edge of the divine?

5. Jesus told his disciples, "Don't let the sharp edge of your expectation get dulled by parties and drinking and shopping." What other instruction does he give us in Luke 21:34 so that we can "make it through everything that's coming"?

6. How do your choices large and small reflect the priorities you *say* you've set for yourself? Are your actions aligned with your priorities?

7. What did Sandi have when she left the bariatric surgeon's office that she didn't have when she arrived? Where did she find it?

Chapter 2. *Living on the Edge*

1. Ephesians 2:7 says God "has us where he wants us." Read the rest of that verse and consider exactly where that "place" is for you right now. Does God have you where he wants you, or are you resisting his guidance?

2. When have you been surprised to realize you've been given a second chance—or a fiftieth? What did you do, or are you doing now, with that opportunity?

3. Has there ever been a time in your life when you could identify with the woman described in John 8:1–8? What did it feel like to be condemned—and then to be released from that situation to "go and sin no more"?

4. Judges 6 tells the story of how Gideon and his small band of warriors were ordered to attack a much larger force. Gideon thought he understood God's orders, but he couldn't be sure. What do *you* do to feel confident you're following God's will in challenging situations?

5. What "fleeces" have you encountered that confirmed for you the choices you were making? What gives you confidence you're living in God's will?

6. Sandi's friend Gene Anderson likes to say, "If you're not living life on the edge, you're taking up too much space!" How does your daily life differ when you're living life on the edge—and when you're not?

7. To Sandi, living on the edge means "constantly watching for new opportunities to connect with

God more intimately, trust him more completely." What opportunities have you experienced recently that you might not have noticed had you been living a more complacent, risk-free life?

8. What does Max Lucado describe as "the supreme force in salvation"? How does it equip us to live life on the edge?

Chapter 3. Edges, Seen and Unseen

1. The prophet Isaiah said it was good that he went through troubles because God held on to his lifeline and "never let me tumble over the edge into nothing" (38:46). Describe a time when God held on to *your* lifeline and kept you from falling.

2. Have there been times in your life when you seemed stuck on the dark side of a hurtful edge, suffering emotional distress, but you didn't seek help? What held you back? How might things have been different for you if you had received counseling?

3. News reports say John Kennedy Jr. "lost the horizon" on a hazy day, and as a result the plane he was piloting crashed into the ocean. Think about how, when you're lost in an emotional fog of confusion, you could find the "edge" that would help keep you on course.

4. Sandi writes that "it's common for abuse victims to seek out people who help us accomplish our subconscious goal." How has judgmental criticism or

other destructive interference kept you or someone you know locked in a prison of harmful behavior or destructive thinking?

5. When Disneyland turned her down for a job with Kids of the Kingdom, Sandi thought her dream of a musical career had ended. What happened instead? How does a "broken road" sometimes lead to greater happiness or success than a direct path?

6. Sandi compares her story to Brer Rabbit's situation— but in reverse. When has God put you in a situation opposite to the circumstances you begged him for— and your life turned out better because of it?

7. Pastor Jim Lyon says he didn't see Sandi crying in the balcony that day in church when he told the congregation God "knows how to find you" even when "all you want to do is sit on the back row of the balcony and cry." Describe a time when someone somewhere has, perhaps unknowingly, said exactly the words you needed to hear. Where do you think those words came from? How does this story encourage you to reach out to those whose hearts are hurting, even when you don't know what to say? (Read Luke 24:12.)

Chapter 4. Finally Valuing My Value

1. What events, words, or situations have led *you* to the "wide open spaces of God's grace and glory" described in Romans 5:1?

2. Through counseling, Sandi learned that "liking what you see in the mirror comes when you realize that *you have value* as a living, breathing human being." What "extraordinarily powerful reason" do Christians have to believe they have value? (Read John 3:16 and Romans 5:8.)

3. In your opinion, what's the difference between having "life" and "having it more abundantly"? (See John 10:10 KJV.)

4. Why is it important to your daily life to recognize that, in God's eyes, your life has great value?

5. What does Sandi mean when she says that "weight loss is an inside job"? What do you do to comfort yourself during tense situations? Are those actions beneficial, or are they destructive habits?

6. Has something in your life evolved from being a "faithful supporter" to a "dominating tyrant," as food did for Sandi? What can you do to take control of that situation?

7. What was the trait that appeared repeatedly in Sandi's personality test results? If someone could review all the challenging situations you've experienced in life, what trait would stand out about your personality? How is your faith related to that trait?

Chapter 5. Seeking the Lost, Cherishing What's Found, Releasing the Excess

1. Have you ever lost something of great monetary or

sentimental value? Describe the feelings that swept over you when you realized the item was lost. How did you handle the loss as time passed?

2. Think of a situation when you searched determinedly for something that was lost, and compare that experience with Jesus' example in Matthew 18:12–14. Now think of *yourself* as the thing that is lost. How do Jesus' words reinforce for you the value God puts on your life?

3. Finish this sentence, which Sandi includes in chapter 5: "Jesus is the most valuable 'possession' we can ever have—because _____."

4. How do we "find" Jesus?

5. How is a journal similar to the rocks the Israelites took out of the Jordan River when they crossed on their way to the promised land? (See Joshua 4:1–22.)

6. In his book, *The Noticer*, Andy Andrews wrote, "The seeds of depression cannot take root in a grateful heart." Why not? (Read Luke 16:8, 1 Thessalonians 5:16–18, and Philippians 4:10.)

7. Let the stories of Sandi's band members inspire you to think of your own story. How did *you* "find" your God-given gifts?

Chapter 6. Hanging on the Cliff-Edge

1. What does "the cliff-edge of doom" look like to you? (Read Psalm 56:1–3, 5–6 to see what it looked like to the psalmist.)

2. When you're going through a difficult life passage, how would Psalm 56:8 provide comfort to you?

3. After the Lap-Band procedure, why did Sandi consider naming her bathroom scale *Isaac*? (See Genesis 47:17, 18:11–13.) What illogical thing in your life makes you laugh because without God it would be so impossible?

4. Sandi imagines herself as Humpty Dumpty, teetering on the wall with a choice of which way she'll fall. On one side she imagines a hearse surrounded by a coroner's crew. On the other side is a team of rescuers waiting beside an ambulance. "And what's that painted on the top of the ambulance? Why, of course! It's a big red _____." For Christians, what's the meaning behind that illustration? Why is the cross symbolic of rescue?

5. Sandi says that overcoming her tendency to second-guess others' hidden messages is helping her "move closer to the edge that separates my past life and the life God wants me to have today." What destructive habit or tendency do you need to overcome to move closer to that life? What's the first step you can take to begin this work? What's the second?

6. Why should we be thankful for the problems we encounter? (Read 1 Thessalonians 5:16 and Job 33:19.) What problem is confronting you now? What would it take for you to be *thankful* for that problem?

7. What did the psalmist say God does for the fallen?

(Read Psalm 147:2, 6.) What did the apostle Paul say we should do instead of worrying? (Read Philippians 4:6–7.)

Chapter 7. Choose Life!

1. When we forget God's promises and find ourselves back in an emotional or spiritual wilderness, what "pile of rocks" should we mentally visit? Why?

2. What "other gods" tempt you away from the healthy, abundant life God wants you to have? How does it help you to identify the circumstances that cause you to stray from the right path?

3. What does God promise to do when we wake up and think, *Dear God, what have I done? Please, Father, can you forgive me?* (Read Isaiah 54:9.)

4. What did Sandi's powerful dream teach her about the power of *choice*? Why do we feel empowered when we have a choice in a difficult situation, even if all available choices are scary?

5. If you could write a musical score to accompany the story of your daily life, how would it impact someone who could hear the music without seeing what happened? Would your music be pleasant or mournful? Uplifting or depressing? Inspirational or discouraging? (Read Psalm 33:1–3.)

6. Read Proverbs 3:5–6. How can we "listen for God's voice" in everything we do? How do we allow him to guide our steps?

7. When Sandi and Don moved to Oklahoma City, their left-behind children felt like their "nest" had disappeared. Have you ever experienced that feeling, as if the foundation of your life had been jerked out from under you? How does *choice* come into play? Contrast this anecdote to what Jesus taught us about the foundation of our faith. (Read Matthew 7:24–29.)

8. Mollie was brokenhearted about having to leave her friends and high school behind and move to Oklahoma City. Sandi and Don told her she didn't have to love her new home or even like it. "You just have to show up every day," they said. What does it mean to "show up every day"? What can we learn from Mollie's example about facing tough challenges and overcoming disappointment? (Read Romans 5:3–5.)

Chapter 8. Enough

1. Sandi told the emergency-room physician, "There just doesn't seem to be enough of me to go around." Why was that such an odd thing for her to say? What does the Bible say is "sufficient" for us to overcome all our weaknesses? (Read 2 Corinthians 12:7–9.)

2. Sandi went from the "top of her game" in the music industry to the floor of a psychiatric hospital, where she huddled amid "profound feelings of failure and shame." Looking back, she is thankful for those sent by God to lead her back to the abundant and

rewarding life God wants her to have. Have you ever felt "like a zero with the rim rubbed out"? Who did God send to help you? When has God sent *you* to someone who needs a listening ear, an encouraging word, or a little act of kindness? How did that experience impact you and the other person?

3. A dictionary defines *enough* as "adequate for the want or need, sufficient." But inspirational speaker Zane Fleming says that *nothing* is ever enough until we understand that _____ is enough. What changes when we understand that truth?

4. Read Romans 5:6. How does it make you feel to realize that God sent his only Son to die for you—even though you are totally useless to him? If God doesn't base our value on what we can *do* for him, why are we worth so much to him?

5. If we are enough for God simply because of his gracious love for us, and if he wants us to love others as he loves us (read John 13:34), how does that affect our relationship with our loved ones? What does it mean to say we accept that they are enough for us and we are enough for them?

6. As Christians, we don't have to be afraid that we'll make a mistake and be lost forever. "We're not just the lost and found," Sandi says. "We're the _____." How many times can we fail and ask God's forgiveness? (Read Matthew 18:24–35.)

7. Jesus said that everything is possible for those who believe. (Read Mark 9:23–24 NIV.) But believing is

sometimes easier said than done. Think about situations when have you struggled to forgive someone who made a mistake. How did you work through that process and do what you knew God wanted you to do?

About Sandi Patty

As one of the most highly acclaimed performers of our time with five Grammy awards, four Billboard Music Awards, three platinum records, five gold records, and eleven million units sold, Sandi Patty is simply known as *The Voice*.

Sandi is the most awarded female vocalist in contemporary Christian music history. With thirty-nine Dove Awards, she was inducted into the Gospel Music Hall of Fame in 2004 and as an Indiana Living Legend in 2007. She has released over thirty albums, including *The Edge of the Divine* (August 2010).

Sandi was introduced to the world with her rendition of "The Star Spangled Banner" during the rededication of the Statue of Liberty in 1986. Virtually overnight she became one of the country's best-loved performers. Her version of the national anthem has become synonymous with patriotic celebration, including performances at A Capitol Fourth with the National Symphony, the Pan American Games, the Indianapolis 500, the dedication of the Francis Scott Key Memorial in Washington, DC, the dedication of Camp David Evergreen Chapel, and ABC's Fourth of July special.

While her thirty-year career is heavily rooted in the gospel music industry, Sandi has had the opportunity in more recent years to extend her career outside the genre. Sandi has performed with symphonies across the country, including the New York Pops, Boston Pops, Cincinnati Pops, Dallas Symphony, Baltimore Symphony, Houston Symphony, and Oklahoma City Philharmonic. Her first pops album, *An American Songbook*, was recorded with the London Symphony Orchestra.

One of Sandi's dreams has been to perform on Broadway, but her commitment to raising her family of eight children always came first. The Indianapolis Symphony Orchestra offered the best of both worlds with "Sandi Patty's Broadway," her 2007 debut feature musical revue.

In addition to her prolific musical career, Sandi is also an accomplished author. For the bestseller *Broken on the Back Row*, Sandi received the 2006 Silver Angel Award. As an author of seven books, her other titles include *Life in the Blender, Falling Forward*, and *Layers*. Her down-to-earth style and sturdy common sense have endeared her to Women of Faith audiences, with whom she has traveled with since 2005. She's an example to all of us of the freedom that comes from learning how to move on, learning from mistakes, and letting God use us in any circumstance.

"I am grateful for the many opportunities God has given in my life and for how he has allowed me to spread my wings," says Sandi. "Singing is my way to tell my story of hope, life, and love."

Sandi and her husband, Don, have eight children. They currently reside in Oklahoma City, Oklahoma.

For more information about Sandi Patty, please visit www.sandipatty.com.

new from WOMEN *of* FAITH

BEAUTIFUL THINGS HAPPEN WHEN A WOMAN TRUSTS GOD

By Sheila Walsh, wherever books are sold

In a message rooted in hope and substantial Bible teaching, Sheila Walsh helps women to see the beautiful things that can happen in their own lives and in the lives of those they love when they fully trust their heavenly Father during good and bad times.

NOTHING IS IMPOSSIBLE

Wherever books are sold

In this Women of Faith devotional, women will encounter page after page of encouragement, humor, insight, and teaching to rediscover the God who will not let them go.

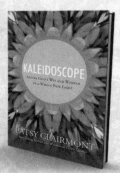

KALEIDOSCOPE

By Patsy Clairmont

Acclaimed author and Women of Faith speaker Patsy Clairmont causes women's hearts to leap and their hopes to lift in this quirky, straight-to-the-point look at the Proverbs.

TELL ME EVERYTHING

By Marilyn Meberg

With the wisdom of a counselor and the wit of a comedian, Marilyn Meberg untangles the issues in women's lives that hold them back from a vibrant relationship with Christ.

FRIENDSHIP FOR GROWN-UPS

By Lisa Whelchel

Former *Facts of Life* star Lisa Whelchel shares her experiences of growing up without true friends, how she learned to find and develop them as an adult through God's grace, and how readers should actively pursue meaningful friendships as adults.

DOING LIFE DIFFERENTLY

By Luci Swindoll

An inspiring account of Luci Swindoll's courageous life that teaches readers how to live savoring each moment, how to let go of regrets, and how to embrace dreams.

THOMAS NELSON
Since 1798